ASPATORE
C-Level Business Intelligence™

Praise for Books, Business Intelligence Publications & Services

"What C-Level executives read to keep their edge and make pivotal business decisions. Timeless classics for indispensable knowledge." - Richard Costello, Manager-Corporate Marketing Communication, General Electric (NYSE: GE)

"Want to know what the real leaders are thinking about now? It's in here." - Carl Ledbetter, SVP & CTO, Novell, Inc.

"Priceless wisdom from experts at applying technology in support of business objectives." - Frank Campagnoni, CTO, GE Global Exchange Services

"Unique insights into the way the experts think and the lessons they've learned from experience." - MT Rainey, Co-CEO, Young & Rubicam/Rainey Kelly Campbell Roalfe

"The Inside the Minds series is a valuable probe into the thought, perspectives, and techniques of accomplished professionals. By taking a 50,000 foot view, the authors place their endeavors in a context rarely gleaned from text books or treatiese." - Chuck Birenbaum, Partner, Thelen Reid & Priest

"Tremendous insights..." - James Quinn, Litigation Chair, Weil Gotshal & Manges

"A must read for anyone in the industry." - Dr. Chuck Lucier, Chief Growth Officer, Booz-Allen & Hamilton

INSIDE THE MINDS

**Empowering Professionals of All Levels
With C-Level Business Intelligence**
www.InsidetheMinds.com

The critically acclaimed *Inside the Minds* series provides readers of all levels with proven business intelligence from C-Level executives (CEO, CFO, CTO, CMO, Partner) from the world's most respected companies. Each chapter is comparable to a white paper or essay and is a future-oriented look at where an industry/profession/topic is heading and the most important issues for future success. Each author has been carefully chosen through an exhaustive selection process by the *Inside the Minds* editorial board to write a chapter for this book. *Inside the Minds* was conceived in order to give readers actual insights into the leading minds of business executives worldwide. Because so few books or other publications are actually written by executives in industry, *Inside the Minds* presents an unprecedented look at various industries and professions never before available.

For information on bulk orders, sponsorship opportunities or any other questions, please email store@aspatore.com.

For information on licensing the content in this book, or any content published by Aspatore, please email jonp@aspatore.com.

To nominate yourself, another individual, or a group of executives for an upcoming Inside the Minds book, or to suggest a specific topic for an Inside the Minds book, please email jason@aspatore.com.

ASPATORE
C-Level Business Intelligence™
Publisher of Books, Business Intelligence Publications & Services

www.Aspatore.com

Aspatore Books is the largest and most exclusive publisher of C-Level executives (CEO, CFO, CTO, CMO, Partner) from the world's most respected companies. Aspatore annually publishes C-Level executives from over half the Global 500, top 250 professional services firms, law firms (MPs/Chairs), and other leading companies of all sizes. By focusing on publishing only C-Level executives, Aspatore provides professionals of all levels with proven business intelligence from industry insiders, rather than relying on the knowledge of unknown authors and analysts. Aspatore Books is committed to publishing a highly innovative line of business books, redefining and expanding the meaning of such books as indispensable resources for professionals of all levels. In addition to individual best-selling business titles, Aspatore Books publishes the following unique lines of business books: Inside the Minds, Business Bibles, Bigwig Briefs, C-Level Business Review (Quarterly), Book Binders, ExecRecs, and The C-Level Test, innovative resources for all professionals. Aspatore Books also provides an array of business services including The C-Level Library, Assemble Your Own Book, SmartPacks, Establish Your Reading Profile, and Build Your Own Library as well as outsourced business library and researching capabilities. Aspatore is a privately held company headquartered in Boston, Massachusetts, with employees around the world.

INSIDE THE MINDS

Inside the Minds:
JumpStart
Launching your Business Venture, Profitably and Successfully

If you are interested in purchasing bulk copies for your team/company with your company logo, and/or licensing this book for a web site, newsletter or other publication, please email store@aspatore.com or call toll free 1-866-Aspatore.

Published by Aspatore, Inc.
For corrections, company/title updates, comments or any other inquiries please email info@aspatore.com.

First Printing, 2003
10 9 8 7 6 5 4 3 2 1

Copyright © 2003 by Aspatore Books, Inc. All rights reserved. Printed in the United States of America. No part of this publication may be reproduced or distributed in any form or by any means, or stored in a database or retrieval system, except as permitted under Sections 107 or 108 of the United States Copyright Act, without prior written permission of the publisher.

ISBN 1-58762-226-2

Inside the Minds Managing Editor, Carolyn Murphy, Edited by Michaela Falls, Proofread by Stephanie Afonso, Cover design by Scott Rattray & Ian Mazie

Material in this book is for educational purposes only. This book is sold with the understanding that neither any of the authors or the publisher is engaged in rendering medical, legal, accounting, investment, or any other professional service. For legal advice, please consult your personal lawyer.

This book is printed on acid free paper.

A special thanks to all the individuals that made this book possible.

The views expressed by the individuals in this book (or the individuals on the cover) do not necessarily reflect the views shared by the companies they are employed by (or the companies mentioned in this book). The companies referenced may not be the same company that the individual works for since the publishing of this book.

Inside the Minds:
JumpStart
Launching your Business Venture, Profitably and Successfully

CONTENTS

Penny Baker, Jr.   **11**
THE FIRST YEAR–MAKE IT OR BREAK IT TIME

James R. Barnes   **25**
*IN STARTING, GROWING & MAINTAINING A
BUSINESS…*

Bob Brennan   **35**
BUILDING YOUR COMPANY

David Carlson   **47**
WHERE TO BEGIN

Bob Carr   **67**
ALL THE RIGHT INGREDIENTS

Richard C. Harshaw   **81**
*INSIDE REALITY VERSUS OUTSIDE
PERCEPTION*

Marina Hatsopoulos 93
PRODUCT DIFFERENTIATION FROM
TECHNOLOGY

Kevin D. Grauman 111
MAKING IT UP AS YOU GO

David R. Cassell 125
ESTABLISHING THE NEED

Bob Lokken 141
THE IMPORTANCE OF VALIDATING YOUR
BUSINESS

Patrick J. Martucci 165
START-UP FUNDAMENTALS

Bent R. Tilson 183
TRAVELING THE ROAD TO REALITY

David Paul Taylor 197
ADAPTING TO YOUR CUSTOMER

Jill Blashack 221
LESSONS LEARNED THROUGH PERSEVERANCE

Doug Harrison **237**

DIVING IN – THE FIRST FEW STEPS ARE THE HARDEST

Acknowledgements & Dedications

The First Year –
Make it or Break it Time

Penny Baker, Jr.
National Bankcard Systems Inc.
President & CEO

Before You Open the Doors

Any entrepreneur must have a high tolerance for risk. That doesn't mean that you ignore strategies to mitigate those risks, but you're going to sleep a lot better if you can live with making decisions when you don't have all the facts - because you'll need to do that. You need to have a high comfort level for ambiguity and risk; in fact, you'd better prefer erring on the side of taking the risk rather than seeking safety. Most of us experience self-doubt from time to time, but remember that someone somewhere can get the job done and that person might as well be you. Once you have done your due diligence, prepare yourself mentally to compete to win and stay focused on that.

Understand that the sales cycle drives any business. Start as a manufacturer's representative and independent broker or in some other position that allows you to master selling to the market you want to reach. Many new business owners think they have to invent something new, but successful entrepreneurs find the unique niche or way to vary something that's already been done. Find something that you can commit to and then make it blossom.

How to Guarantee Failure – or Success

You are destined to fail if you ignore your business, even just a little bit, during your first year. You absolutely must be committed 24/7 to watch everything, learn everything and do it all.

In order to succeed, you need to wear all the hats and understand every role in the company. Never rely on somebody else, especially in the beginning. You need to master every job in your company so that you can teach others, and you can tell immediately if someone needs retraining or something needs to change. There's no other way for you to thoroughly comprehend your operation than to literally work in every position. It's your company and no one has more to lose – or gain – so be prepared to act accordingly.

Although you should communicate your enthusiasm for the business with everyone in your company, it's unrealistic to think that anyone will experience this at the same level that you do. To expect this of your staff only breeds disappointment and resentment on their part and yours. Be passionate, but find a balance. If you go too far, you can come across as abrasive and overbearing, and you'll lose your people.

Many new businesses have a difficult time succeeding because the CEO has to be good at more than one thing, and often is exceptionally skilled in one area, but not the others. Just because you are a great salesperson doesn't necessarily make you a great leader, and if you are a great leader, it doesn't necessarily make you good with money. All of those things are equally important and you need to shore up your skills where necessary.

Additionally, people often do not understand what it takes to make payroll and other overhead. There is a constant struggle with cash flow and expenses, even if you have great ideas and great concepts. Sometimes there seems to be plenty of money in the bank, and then a month or two later you have a couple thousand dollars in the bank account with thirty-five thousand in payroll. At times like this, you'd better scramble to get your plan together. Look at every possible avenue for generating one more sale, getting one more lease funded, collecting on one more receivable, or any other possible method of speeding up the wheel. If this won't cut it, then you need to look into available funds on credit cards or finding other avenues of bringing cash into the company.

Stay focused on the fundamentals. All business owners should look at two things when they get to work in the morning: the book balance and the bank balance. Their book balance is what they have out in checks or what their payables are, and their bank balance is what they actually have in the checking account. If you've got a positive in the checking account, and you look like you can manage your book balance in terms of what your payables and your receivables are, then it's a good day. I think if you look at it on a grander scale than that, especially with your own company, it can be overwhelming. You don't know what tomorrow holds, and it is a struggle everyday. This is the reason, in my opinion, that so many over-funded companies went out of business. They were looking at the big picture and market share and all these things that don't pay the light bill today. Pay attention to cash flow daily. If you need new office furniture, only buy it when you have the money. What you don't want to do is bank on tomorrow's sale to make today's purchase. Don't buy in advance of need.

Business plans, in my opinion, are usually meaningless. They are great in terms of trying to borrow money and secure investors. They help people around you or people associated with your company to have confidence in what you are doing, because it makes you look like you are on the ball and that you have put a lot of effort into forecasting your business. But from what I've witnessed with successful entrepreneurs, they change the business plan ten times a month anyway. What you thought was going to get you to the "promised land" is altogether different from what it is going to be three days from now, three months from now and six months from now. It changes so fast, and so much of it is trial and error. This is the beauty of not being over-funded. When you are a start-up business with little investment capital and you are building it from your sales, if something is not working you have to change course really fast. The need for correction becomes obvious right away – it can't hide behind funding. You can write a business plan and make sales projections and those sorts of things, and anybody worth their salt in business can tell you that you need to do them, but you must be prepared to deviate from those things when you have to.

You can stay on track in terms of your core focus and your mission-critical areas, but in order to grow your business, you also must have 100 percent confidence in yourself that you are going to get the job done; be willing to do whatever it takes to get the job done; and remain flexible and creative in finding a way to keep your business afloat. This doesn't mean that if you're selling credit card terminals one day, all of a sudden you start building Websites – you have to "stay within the headlights." But in terms of a business plan and how you are going to reach your goals, that is going to deviate from your initial plan almost every day. For example, be open to pursuing a new niche within your industry. Once you decide to go after that niche, march out there and do it with a bang. Get there first and call everyone in the country. Quickly establish yourself as the market leader and get those phones ringing.

What's Unique About the First Year?

When it's just you out there selling your product or service you'll probably achieve a higher closing ratio. Don't be fooled into thinking that your sales staff will accomplish the same sales statistics that you can. It's not as simple as thinking, "I can close twenty sales per week, so if I hire three sales reps, they should be able to do sixty sales per week." It just doesn't work that way. Your sales efforts will become diluted as you turn your attention to the task of operating the business. Human resource issues such as hiring and terminating, developing employee handbooks and purchasing office workstations, and a thousand other things will require more of your time as the company grows.

Be realistic with your sales projections when it's someone other than you in front of the customer. Although some may come close, remember that no one will share your same level of passion and that can work to your advantage in front of the customer. Don't lose sight of this edge, and make yourself available to accompany the sales representatives on sales calls. When you help them close a tough sale you put money in their pocket, and they learn how to do it for themselves the next time around. Especially during the first year, keep yourself visible and available to the sales team that is building your business. And keep yourself in front of your customers, because you need to hear what they have to say. It means something to them to deal with the owner. Don't ever get so busy with other things that you don't have time to talk with your customers.

Sell or Die

When you're just starting out you need salespeople that can hit the ground running. Don't waste your time with someone who hasn't already proven their value in your industry or a situation where the skills will transfer easily. If your salespeople need to make cold calls, then only hire someone who has figured out how to win in that environment. If your product is highly technical, only hire reps that have sold highly technical products. If your market is specialized, hire people that know how to talk to that group effectively. You can't afford to spend your first year teaching people how to sell – you'll have your hands full teaching them the intricacies of your product, and you don't want to hold their hand through the sales process.

Your company must have sales to keep the doors open. You have to prove yourself every day in business and you have to get a sale everyday. From day one I have tried to stress the mentality that "sales is a today business." Not only the sales reps, but also all of the employees in your company must have that frame of mind. What are you going to do today? You have to earn your pay everyday. How are you going to do that? You have to make a sale, get a check, or get a lease funded. You have to keep the money going and that happens through consistent effort every single day. Focus your sales team on making "x" number of new contacts each and every day. The numbers will work if they keep the pipeline full. If they don't make this effort everyday, and it's tough on the days when sales are coming in, they'll come up empty-handed a few weeks from now because they let the pipeline dry out. You cannot operate a profitable business this way. Just stay focused on precisely what you are going to do everyday, and everything else falls into place.

One of the biggest stumbling blocks in starting a new business is that you are entering into a very competitive arena. You have to know what the market will withstand and what the market will bear. Anything short of that and you will probably go out of business. In free enterprise, it is kind of like the Serengeti: the weak will get squashed. Know your competition. Call every possible competitor and walk in the shoes of their customers. Purchase their product if you need to because the investment will be worth the knowledge you gain. You're making a huge mistake if you don't do this. Share this insight with your sales staff and teach them how to position your company in the marketplace.

Remember, you are the company's best salesperson. Although you'll spend a lot of time in front of your customers, as the CEO your priority customer is your sales force. Keep them sold on and excited about your product or service. Their state of mind and mental sharpness makes and breaks sales everyday. Help them to become more successful than even they imagine for themselves. Do this by providing them with information on the competition, insight to the customer base and marketplace, and staying in the trenches with them. They'll respect you for it and they'll learn from you. Never miss an opportunity to equip them with the skills to handle one more objection. Spend an hour everyday role-playing, overcoming objections. This might sound like a lot of time out of the selling day, but a well-prepared sales staff goes out there and makes money. A salesperson that stumbles because they do not have the right information, tools, or training throws money out the window with every missed opportunity.

INSIDE THE MINDS

Communication is key. Keep them involved and informed. Do everything that you can in the way of incentives, bonuses, and profit sharing. The greater their sense of ownership, the greater their investment and, therefore, effort.

The Human Factor

In your first year, you can't afford to bring in anyone, sales person or otherwise, looking for a 9 to 5 job. You have to get people excited and show them how the dream of your company will apply to them. If you hire a 60-year-old corporate veteran, not only is he accustomed to a puffed-up benefits package, for example, he's also heard it all already. While he may possess valuable skills, he's an unlikely fit for your start-up company. Look for those individuals that want to work early and late and have a hunger for success. It's better to hire someone with one failure under their belt instead of a recent graduate that believes all the propaganda they were told about what they should expect because of their newly-minted degree. You want the guy that got cheated out of a great job and has something to prove – someone hungry for the opportunity to show what he or she can do.

Stay away from people who provide a rash of excuses for the reason they left their previous job. You have no time for whiners or people who can't accept personal responsibility. Don't waste time or resources this first year or you won't make it.

If you want to be successful, treat others like you want to be treated. You read in the *Wall Street Journal* and business publications about the way certain companies treat their employees, and how it's a big family and how they have a special room for yoga and all of these things that are often just a little bit of smoke. Who cares about that? People are very smart in terms of knowing if you respect them. You can spot it a mile

18

THE FIRST YEAR – MAKE IT OR BREAK IT TIME

away if there is a little disrespect. It's as keen as a dog's instinct about a stranger. Treat people the way you want to be treated - with respect.

Employees are your greatest asset or the greatest potential liability. With entrepreneurs, by nature, it's just go, go, go. You have your eye on the next sale. You think everything is going to work and you think, "This is great. I can't believe I'm going to be so successful." You just expect everything to work out. So when somebody sits in front of you interviewing for a job, you want to give everybody a chance. But you can't do that. Think about it. You'll talk to twenty to fifty people to get just one sale, but a lot of entrepreneurs will hire the next person who walks in the door. In terms of getting good people, it is a numbers game too. It is a process like anything else. The more you put into it in terms of resources, time, and effort, the more you get out of it. Even with the best hiring effort, it is still trial and error. If the person doesn't work out, don't waste any time in turning them loose. Do it quickly, but kindly. You are doing nobody a favor by keeping them on.

Your hiring practices determine your employee situation. At the end of the day, the people who are going to be good employees are the ones who are good people from within. What are my obligations to the employee? If I promise that I am going to give him a check for a dollar amount twice a month, then that money has to be there. If I don't give him a check, or the check bounces at the bank, how long are those guys going to stick around? If I don't fulfill my end of the obligation, they are not going to be around. Yet there are a lot of employees that feel that because they have done a great job for a while, they can put it on cruise control for a little bit. If I tried to do that with them, they would kick me to the curb and go work for somebody else. You have to do your due diligence in the people that you hire and only hire those that have personal integrity and a strong work ethic.

I don't think it's a good idea to hire any friends or family. By nature, you think in terms of loyalty and friendship, but this doesn't always translate to business. It sounds great in concept, but it doesn't necessarily apply. You put both the business and the relationship at risk, and it's not worth it. There is something valuable and less risky about keeping business and personal lives separate.

If interviewing and hiring isn't your passion, be sure that when you can afford to do so, you carefully hire someone for whom this is a passion. Counterbalance your weaknesses with someone else's strengths.

The Real Boss

Without the customer you have no income. Lose sight of this and you lose, especially your first year. Return phone calls. This is so crucial yet it's amazing how many busy CEOs let this slip. And don't just focus on new business – take care of your repeat customers. Watch out, because although they have a higher threshold for the "pain" of waiting to hear back from you, if you make your existing customers wait, you leave the door wide open for your competition to rush in.

Naturally you're going to miss some calls while you're running around putting your business together, but you must always return the calls that day. Even an evening message on voice mail shows that you made the attempt and creates a different tone for the call on the next day. If you take customer service a small percentage further than your competition, your customers will notice. For example, I spent two nights in a hotel and could immediately determine that two different housekeepers had tended to my room each night. Which one do you want working for you? The first night my room was cleaned well, and I had fresh linens waiting when I returned that evening. The second night, I enjoyed the same experience, but this housekeeper took about twenty seconds to make a lasting impression. She carefully lined up my razor, shaving cream, and other toiletries on a folded white washcloth. It's so easy to do just a little bit more. You need to take advantage of every opportunity to build the "little things" into your customer care.

During your first year you must concentrate on things that lend credibility. If you are a reseller of a product or service provided by an established company, put that out front. Your company may be as yet unproven, but you can boost confidence through your affiliation with a more mature enterprise.

Think twice about signing a lease for cheap space. An office in your city's central business district provides you with an instant "good impression" and the opportunity to showcase that building prominently on your Web site, brochures, and other marketing and communications materials. First impressions do count, especially when you're trying to establish your company's identity. The same strategy applies to anyone that meets your customers. Do what the "big guys" in your industry do. If you're competing against guys in sharp suits and ties – you'd better put on the same show.

Keep the Doors Open

It's surprising how many entrepreneurs don't understand the concept of cash flow. It's really simple: the money going out has to be just a little bit less than the money coming in. Just because you make a sale or an agreement and you send an invoice, that doesn't necessarily put money into your checking account. In business, you are always spending money to grow the company, whether it is through human resources, marketing, advertising or direct mail. You have to have a really good grasp of what is coming in and what is going out. I had a friend who just started his own law practice. He previously was a partner in a law firm, and he thought that when the invoices went out, the checks would start coming in. That's a whole other business in and of itself, managing your receivables.

Just as you monitor your cash flow, watch how you spend your time. While you need to get out and meet all the prospects you can, at industry events, for example, people just sit around and talk about nothing. I think that there are very few people that really get something out of it. For the most part, it is a huge waste of time. They all say that they are networking, but they are not selling anything. And remember that making sales happen now is what will make or break your business, especially in the first year. I think you have to be really careful in terms of the networking world. The dot com world was full of it. They were all networking and doing trade ops, but no one was accomplishing anything TODAY. You may get lucky with a contact, but in my opinion this is usually a time consuming way to make a sale.

You will become inundated with calls from people saying that they are a local business owner in town with a client who might be interested in your service, and you should meet with them so that they can start referring their customers to you. This also can be a huge waste of time. You'll also hear from friends who got into insurance or real estate and are always trying to sell you something. I don't like that avenue. If you really want to go somewhere with your business, you don't need to sell all your friends and family in order to get there. Once again, it is keeping the professional and personal aspects of your life at an arm's length apart. If you want to be successful, you will have to generate business on your own. With the whole networking thing through friends and family, a lot of times they want something for nothing and will have unrealistic expectations compared to the average consumer. That, and you put the relationship at risk. It's just not a good idea.

THE FIRST YEAR – MAKE IT OR BREAK IT TIME

In general, if you are starting a business, you end up taking advice from your parents or your close friends or a professor, but for the most part, none of these people have ever done it. All of these people are giving you advice, and they haven't done it! If they have been employed with another company, and never taken the risk of starting a business, how are these people really going to help you? It is so easy to use clichés and say "think outside the box" and so on, but as well meaning as they may be, you have to disregard what everybody is telling you. The thing that helped me a lot is that I bought and read many business books and case studies. Learning from people who have actually done it. I think that is what is so valuable about a MBA. I don't have a college degree; in fact, I graduated in the bottom quarter of my high school class but I read my share of business stories. When you get an MBA, you review a lot of case studies, and that is exactly what I did. Be willing to study and learn something new each and every day. But learn from those that have succeeded at what you are setting out to do.

Finally, don't get rattled. You can have some big swings, and believe it or not, the highs can be just as dangerous as the lows. When things are good, don't read too much into it, and remember to keep filling that pipeline. Business moves in cycles, so when things are bad, don't read too much into that either. Keep working, pay attention to your business, and don't let the challenges get you down. Remember, you can look at business as one big game, so play to win, stay focused on the things that will help you to do that. And remember to do those things every day.

Penny Baker Jr. is president and chief executive officer of Austin, Tex.-based National Bankcard Systems, Inc. A natural entrepreneur, Baker thrives on risk and enjoys carrying the responsibility for his decisions. In business since 1997, Baker's company is one of the fastest growing in the country and earned the No. 27 spot on Inc magazine's 2002 list of America's 500 fastest-growing private businesses. In the past, a ranking on the Inc 500 has often been an early indicator of future accomplishments on a global scale. Companies that have made the list include Microsoft, Oracle, Gateway and Domino's Pizza.

National Bankcard Systems provides credit card processing, point-of-sale terminals, online "shopping cart systems," check verification, collection and electronic check conversion for small to midsize businesses throughout the United States.

In Starting, Growing & Maintaining a Business...

Don't Take No for an Answer

James R. Barnes
OAKLEAF Waste Management
Founder and President

Important Tactics for Starting a Business

To start a business, you must have determination to survive. No matter what happens, you are going to get to the next day and keep moving. I look back and forward to some of these challenges like a huge wave coming at you in the surf; you just put your arms together, hold your breath, and dive through it and come up on the other side. There is a lot of distraction, and there are a lot of nay-sayers who say that it can't be done, or that it is foolish, or that it is not viable. If you really believe in your business and push hard, then you will make believers of others.

It is very important to have goals as a company. We have always had lofty goals, and we have come very close to hitting those goals nearly all the time. They are quite incredible. We have grown at 6,300 percent over the last five years. We thrive on keeping up with the pace. By sharing that goal with all of the people here and then giving them the incentive to help get there, that gets them all into the game. I truly believe that everybody has to have a piece of the action. They have to have an incentive to hit the big goal. By hitting these goals we grow faster than our competition, gain scale, maximize leverage with price and service, and effectively put more to the capital infrastructure or bottom line over time.

In the early days of this business, we tried to build a lot of excitement by getting one success and coupling that to the next one and the next one and keeping it going. We let everyone know when we had a small victory. We would mail out announcements to a 3,000-person database of contacts as we landed each client. People would get a mailer three or four times each month. It gave the perception that we were getting a lot of clients. We also put that into our advertising – saying that in the last 90 days or 120 days we had added the following clients. It actually listed them, which was kind of a bold move. Some people would be afraid of the competition knowing that. On our side, though, knowing that we were comfortable in our position with the clients and proud of what we were doing and confident, it really made a bold statement. That really started building traction. I remember going to a trade show sometime in the third year of business and the buzz from all of the prospects was exactly that. Several prospects mentioned that it seemed as if they received one of our postcards every other day.

I also searched out all avenues to find people who could help me reach the right decision-makers. If I knew somebody who had leads into a certain industry, I would approach them to see if they could help me. We did a lot of leveraging of relationships to get into other doors and avenues. If you can gain trust from someone where they are confident that you will do the right thing and be successful with their relationship, then you can get a quick jump into some deals that you normally wouldn't get into until you were more formally established. New clients take a risk when they sign up with a new company, therefore they need to wholeheartedly believe you are going to do what you say, and if you make a mistake, which you inevitably will, you will get it corrected quickly and get it done right.

Management and Leadership

This management team evolved. It was originally just me, and I didn't have any money whatsoever to assemble a dream team. But as time goes on and you start to generate even a little bit of cash flow you need to take every dollar you possible can and put it back in to hire the best person you can. Every time you have an opportunity to hire somebody who is as good as or better than you are, even if it costs more money, it is probably worth it to do it in the initial years. It will pay off later on. Rather than taking that bonus or that increase in salary, leverage it. Hire somebody who is actually better or more expensive than you are.

I'm very driven and very persistent. I see a way through everything. Everybody who works for me knows that if there is an obstacle, we are going to overcome it, and if it's something that can't be done, we are going to find a way to do it. I think part of that is driven by speed. I like to move quickly. If you can outflank your competition because you are working seven days a week and they are only working five, it will start to benefit your side. Most of my competitors don't work more than a 40-hour week. If I have people who are motivated by bonuses to go above and beyond, then they get to see the fruits of their labor. And on the client side, they see that extra effort and they see the value in that, and they stay with you. The numbers add up. If you have ten people that work ten extra hours every week, that extra hundred hours a week (5,200 hours/year) is like having three additional full-time people. In a small company that could be a 30 percent gain in work force and most of the companies don't do this because there is no focus on what they are trying to accomplish.

I think the other key is that I really try to delegate. I realize that I can't know every little thing about the company. I can't process every invoice, and I can't have every client relationship. I need to trust that to other people, and I really stress that to my management. I challenge my managers: "What would happen if you weren't here tomorrow? Who would be doing your work for you? How are you going to advance up from where you are unless you find somebody to fill your shoes?" A lot of that stems from the dreaded question it seems was always coming for the first several years from prospects who would say, "Well this all sounds great but what happens if you get hit by a truck."

When you are building a company at this speed, you are constantly recruiting from within your ranks to find better people along the way. You have to be very focused on keeping the talent and the level of expertise growing. Just because somebody was here two or three years ago and they had a certain position, it doesn't mean that they are going to have that next year when we are hiring better people, and other people can do the job better than they can. They need to perform at an ever growing and a challenging level. It is difficult to make those calls, especially when you are a very small company and you start to grow up. You need to groom the people who can be groomed, and you need to try to find the people who can't handle the new challenges and find other positions for them. I keep challenging the employees. It's kind of like the saying; that if you have an important job that has to get done then you give it to the person whom is the busiest because they will probably get it done. When somebody shows by example that they have the ability to take on additional challenges and execute them, I want to give them more opportunities and let them grow. I have some amazing associates who just continue to out do themselves. They stretch, they grow, they gain confidence and then they grab more real estate. It is fascinating to witness, especially when they spread the culture and you see the people under their guidance start to do the same.

I don't think people are born leaders, but I think that some people develop a knack for it. I think a leader needs to build on success – and on little successes. Leaders need to make sure that they are constantly rallying and supporting employees and that they are encouraging them and challenging them. As long as the people who work with you see that and know that there is that type of activity, they feel part of it. At the end of the day, all anybody really wants, is to be part of a winning team. Money is nice. It is definitely important to pay the bills, but it doesn't put a tiger in your belly. It doesn't make you jump out of bed like being on a winning team does.

I try to find positive people – people who believe in themselves, people who believe in a mission, and people who find a way to get a job done. Those are the kind of people who will find a solution. I think you need a driving force and a mission to rally around in order to build a successful team. No one is here to accomplish what we were going to accomplish last year or the year before. They share the vision that we are building this company to be the best and the largest in our segment, and we are trying to do it at a level that is 20 times the size of our closest competitor. That underlining theme is what drives people in their mission every day at work.

A tough thing about being a leader is that you need to make some very hard calls, and you need to live or die with those decisions. You either have a stomach for that or you don't. Some of the toughest calls are when you truly need to pass over somebody who can't keep up anymore, or you have people who have done a good job but not a great job, and there are better opportunities for the whole company if you move those people out and bring in people who can do it better. A lot of business people talk about this. Its easy to talk about, its another thing to make the call.

Thinking about the "what-ifs" still keeps me up at night. We have been on a fairly aggressive acquisition program, and that involves financing, due diligence, and deal making. That keeps me up. I wonder if the conversion process or the transition process will go as well as I want.

I am also always thinking about what other competitors might do. It is not just waiting around to see what they will do or waiting to react to them – it is thinking about all of the things that they could do and beating them to that option before they can execute. If they are going to try to build a competitive advantage, how can we surpass them? How can we beat them to the punch?

Gaining and Retaining Customers

When we started, we were in a small 10 x 10 office in a stable at a horse-riding ranch. We moved somewhere else the next year and somewhere else the year after that. I finally had a potential client who said that they would like to come out and see the operation. They were from the West, and they wanted to come all the way out East to see us. I said, "Sure, why not?" and quickly started fixing the place up. They came in late, and we stayed late – probably until six or seven o'clock at night – because their plane was delayed. The next day they said that the most incredible part of the operation was the system, but also the people, and that we should show it to everyone. From that point on, that became our proposition model. Now we challenge anyone to take our offer. We will fly them to see our operation, and we will even fly them to see our competitors, on our nickel. That has turned into about a 90 percent success rate of clients who come to see us and eventually sign up with us. That is because they get to see the people, and they feel the excitement that is going on in the operation. They see some pretty incredible systems and they gain comfort in that. The best salesperson cannot relay the excitement that comes from seeing 230 people who are "on a mission". That is a resource that we have capitalized on. We also identified that as a weakness of our competitors. We knew that many of them didn't have those systems. Once potential clients came to see us, we would tell them to be sure to ask about this and that when they went to see the competition. Now when they meet the competition they are a very educated prospect and they know what to ask.

We need to constantly raise the bar in terms of customer service. We need to make sure that every call is the best call of the day that we make. We need to overachieve. We need to under-promise and over-deliver. You hear a lot of those phrases and read about them in customer service statements, but at the end of the day it comes down to attention to detail. When somebody calls because something didn't happen, are you making sure that you take care of it for him or her before you leave the building? Fortunately, we've built systems that are able to track that and show us who is doing what, where and how long it took and who missed the most, and so on. At the end of the day, it is that human who has to make the call and to make sure that the person on the other line trusts them and believes that they are doing the best that they can to get it done. This goes back to the beginning about gaining trust and confidence from a prospect. When someone can believe that the person on the other side of the phone or email is going to take charge of this situation all the way until its concluded, that's when you gain confidence from your customer and they don't want to think about working with someone else. Nobody today has time to go back and double check to get things done. They find real value in being able to trust someone to get the job done.

If you take the advice of somebody who has mostly an analytical mind, say a bean counter, then they say that certain customers take a lot of our time and they are not as profitable as these other ones, and if we cut them then we might save some money. You can go through this analysis, but at the end of the day, if you lose that customer, they will tell somebody else that they no longer work with you and this can result in a negative reaction. I look at every little transaction as a very important part of the business. I think that from an entrepreneurial standpoint, we don't want to lose any customers. There are many big companies that gain customers and then they lose them, and they just keep thinking that they will back-fill with new customers and raise the rates on the other ones, and they will make up for it. That is not a long-term strategy. It costs far more to gain a client than it does to retain them. We still have our first customer. That is our best testimonial. There are people that we have grown to work with as a result of this first customer of ours who has literally told hundreds of potential clients how we do. It's simple math. A happy customer tells five people and a disgruntled former customer tells twenty. In our company the sales person has always closed the sale and the account manager then manages the account. (There is a definite skill set of people that sell best and a definite skill set of people that manages relationships best.) In the very beginning as it is today, I am constantly telling prospects and clients that at any time I want to be able to ask an account manager to call on any customer for a reference. If the

IN STARTING, GROWING & MAINTAINING A BUSINESS...

answer is no, the question is why, and then how long will it be before we can use them as a reference.

In this competitive market environment I think everybody works harder at what they do for a little bit less than what they used to get. I think that is just business today. Today, our business is focused on volume more than ever. It is important for us to be the largest customer of our local vendor. That helps us to get the best service in the marketplace.

I think our business has changed – it is more technologically driven. Ten years ago, a lot of people still didn't have fax machines, whereas now we are focusing on who doesn't have an Internet connection. We have very developed computer systems. We are processing tens of thousands of invoices, mostly electronically through EDI, which saves us a tremendous amount of money. We spent the money up front, whereas a lot of our smaller competitors haven't been able to pull that together.

I think that when the public markets return to a favorable position, there will be a rebound of the consolidation cycle that occurred in the 1980s and 90's. The segment we are in, which is waste management services or waste management brokerage, is consolidating at a rapid rate. I think this will be the wave of the future.

If you spend your time listening and reacting and building and making it easier for the client to do business with you, then you are doing all the right things. If you are doing all those things, then the client will stay. They will stick with you. They like what they get from you. The profitability and the client base and everything else will build from that. In doing that, all of your employees are focused on that as your critical mission. That is the right place to be focused on. If you are just focused on profitability from day one, you might as well be an accountant. You might not have a business. If you can focus on building a service that a client can't live without or one in which it would be very difficult for the

33

INSIDE THE MINDS

client to go elsewhere, then you are building something. That is where it begins.

One of my favorite sayings and beliefs is that perception is reality. If you can give your clients the perception that what you are building is the very best and the most capable, and it is very driven, then they will see that. They latch onto it, and they are a part of it. Just like associates who want to be part of a winning team, clients too take great pride in being a part of the excitement and success of a growing company.

James R. Barnes is the founder and president of OAKLEAF Waste Management, which he grew from beginnings in 1995 to the $200 Million National Waste Management Service Company it is today. Barnes was awarded a B.S. in Business Administration from Marist College in Poughkeepsie NY in 1984. Previous to founding OAKLEAF, Barnes served as Director of Marketing for Coldwell Banker Residential Real Estate and was a Partner in Downtown Development Corporation. Barnes resides in Hartford, CT with his wife Donna and two children, Lauren and Clayton.

Building Your Company

Bob Brennan
Connected Corporation
President & CEO

Starting a Company

Starting a business is a little bit crazy. An entrepreneur is willing to essentially start with nothing but a vision and execute against that vision despite ridiculous odds. There is an element of faith that exists in an entrepreneur's constitution that is hard to describe but that manifests itself in unbridled energy, eternal optimism, a sense of destiny, and hopefully a sense of humor. Starting a business is hard work.

The key in starting a company is to make sure that the business you are starting is built around a customer problem – a problem that you know if you solve it can bring you high value – and therefore extract money from the customer in exchange for your product or services. The key is to focus on a problem that has a high cost to the potential customer and low value – for example, something that they really don't feel should be taking a lot of their time but, nonetheless, takes a lot of their money. If you can reduce their costs associated with that problem, you can provide a lot of value in exchange for taking it off their hands by bringing a solution to bear on that.

Then, in looking at the total available market, you have to ask if the market you are addressing is large enough to support an independent company, or if it is simply a niche. Then you look at your product strategy or service strategy for addressing that market and solving the customer pain or problem – you need to be able to articulate it in words that anyone can understand.

The third step is assembling a team. The team is a critical part of any venture's success. Do you have the right domain expertise for that market? Do you have the right people in place so that you can scale the company, and you are not constantly upgrading or replacing them? Is there chemistry between the initial team? Without chemistry you are almost doomed, even if your market is large and your product strategy is

BUILDING YOUR COMPANY

correct. If the first few people working together as a team are not operating with alignment and a strong sense of interplay, they will be in tough shape.

Successful entrepreneurs are usually successful over many ventures. During their career, they establish a cadre of people that they work with that want to follow them. The key is attracting people you know you can work with and you have experience with. If you are going into it on your own, without really having access to a team you have built up in your career, the odds against you go up significantly. But if you have people that you know have domain experience in the areas you are seeking and that have worked with you before, they will want to work with you because they feel you will be successful. It is really a matter of your past.

For a team to be successful you need a common vision and transparency of information between all the team members. You need to make sure that anybody who is a jerk gets off the team fast. The other thing that is important is to constantly air areas where there is not alignment so you can get alignment. Misalignment is so costly to a small company. You can have misalignment in a large company because you have the inertia of the market working for you. That inertia does not exist in a start-up.

The next major area to address after the team would be to make sure that you have a sober financial plan that is steeped in reality and recognizes that virtually everything takes longer than you think it will and is built around those contingencies.

The last area I look at when evaluating a start-up or contemplating a start-up is examining the extent to which you can get others to help you. To what extent can you get leverage in the areas of choice through partnerships? The right partnership can multiply your efforts and help your company get more done with the same amount of energy. Good partnerships provide business leverage.

37

The most important things involved in writing a business plan have very little to do with writing it and everything to do with understanding how you are going to approach this market differently than other people who are in it. How is your strategy going to uniquely solve a problem that is not being solved today? How can you compensate for the weaknesses of the team, the threats that come from competitors, and the things that invariably go wrong when starting a company? In other words, do not think that you have it right. Make sure you understand that if you get the market right and you get the team right and you have the finances necessary to make mistakes in that first six months to a year, you will be fine. The biggest mistake I see with business plans is that they are incredibly thought through – they are detailed and have all kinds of charts, forecasts, and analysis – but they are based on bad data. It is basically bad data on top of bad data, so you end up with a very attractive looking plan that has little to do with reality. I would keep it as simple as possible and focus on those three key areas.

Getting the Venture off the Ground

The most successful technique for getting a new venture off the ground is to get people invested in your success prior to forming the company. Many times these people are referred to as an advisory board. As you are contemplating starting the venture, you must figure out who would be the potential buyers of this and do what you can to get an audience and describe how you perceive the problem, how you would go about solving it, and how it would be of value. Then get those key influencers in the audience you are targeting to essentially help guide your course, because that invests them in your success. The most important thing to do is to get validation and not simply trust your opinion.

Don't spend too much. Treat nickels like they are manhole covers. Entrepreneurs are naturally optimistic. They in turn anticipate demand

and build up infrastructure in anticipation of demand, when in fact they should build up infrastructure in reaction to demand. Don't spend your money before you have your revenue. Remember that there are two kinds of problems for entrepreneurial endeavors: lack of revenue and all the other problems. The biggest thing that can help you as you start out is to land that first customer. Then you can focus on successfully deploying that customer so they can act as a reference for you with other prospects. But the most important thing a new company can do is to ring that cash register.

I don't think there is any seminal moment in which you can say, "Ah-ha! We are underway." Too many entrepreneurs think that the ah-ha comes when you have landed your first account. A start-up is a fragile enterprise and it needs to be handled as such. Everything will take longer than you expect. You will not have the money you would like to do all the things you would like to do. The customers will be more demanding than seems fair or prudent, given how much money you have for your product or service. I think it is hubris to think that you are underway until the time when you are actually making money.

The Role of the CEO

The CEO has a single job, and that is to manage people. You have to manage your board members, your management team, the people two levels down in your organization, the prospects, the customers, and the potential partners. It is all about people management. Much of it comes back to the CEO's personality, especially in the early going. As CEO, you must attract the stakeholders to your vision and what you are trying to accomplish. The worst thing a CEO can do is to be inaccessible to his people. Introverted CEOs are, from my perspective, doomed.

The key is to be aware of what from your original vision works and what does not. Make sure that you are shoring up those weaknesses and exploiting your strengths. You should be constantly refining your value proposition from the perspective of: here is the pain that we look to erase, here is how we go about doing it, here is why it is efficient, and here is why you should consider its usefulness. You constantly reinforce a consistent message. As a small start-up you are "n" number of people against the world. You need to make sure that those few people you have on your side are singing the exact same song from a value-proposition perspective.

The CEO's job is basically making bad vs. bad decisions. Good vs. bad and good vs. good should be left to others because they are fairly obvious decisions. By definition, entrepreneurs are risk takers. The key in taking a risk is to be comfortable being wrong. It is fine to take risks with your company, your finances, your product, and your customer base as long as you are comfortable reversing yourself should you prove to be wrong. Too many entrepreneurs are very bight people who are too interested in being right when right isn't necessarily relevant. What is relevant is making sure that you succeed.

Self-awareness is the most important characteristic of a strong leader. You must recognize what you do well and, more importantly, recognize what you do not do well. Good leaders are comfortable with not having all the answers and with being wrong. Leaders are willing to take risks and they make sure that their people know they care. Anyone can learn the textbook characteristics of a successful leader, but self-awareness, confidence, enthusiasm, caring, and transparency are characteristics that I am not sure that anybody can acquire.

The most difficult thing about being a manager is how you spend your time. Am I better off talking to an employee who I know is in distress or a prospect that I know I could potentially buy this month? Should I spend

BUILDING YOUR COMPANY

my time listening to a partner who is angry at a tactical incident? It is really choosing your priorities, such that you always map them back to the relationships. So you look at the relationships that are most important to you and then leverage those relationships. It is very easy for a CEO to get caught up in the incidental contact or tactics that come up in running a company, but what is important for a leader is to focus on the major objectives of the company and move the company in that direction.

I know I have succeeded as an entrepreneur if we have built a company that is recognized as an industry standard and an industry leader, and it is a company comprised of strong, caring, hard-working people who are known as really good people to work with. To create wealth for those people and for our investors, and to make that wealth an extraordinary amount of wealth would be very satisfying. You can look across and know that you have financed thousands of college educations because you have gone past the start-up phase and you are now a successful large company, and you have produced stellar returns for your investors and people are enjoying a quality of life that they otherwise couldn't have.

Dealing with Change

Our company was started just prior to the formation of the Internet bubble, so the company has seen the roller coaster of the Internet bubble and the follow-on hangover. When the company was started, companies that produced profit and solved problems were of value. As the company entered its formative year of getting customers to adopt and apply its solutions, companies that lost money and showed great promise as a function of miracles occurring had great value, and there was less value applied to companies that were solving real problems. The good news for us is that it all came home to roost and solving real business problems and funding growth out of your own earnings is in vogue again. I think it is in vogue permanently now, at least for the software industry.

41

INSIDE THE MINDS

During a turbulent economy the most important thing is to be as transparent as possible about the state of the business. We have to be careful to point out the realities of the environment, but also to point out the benefits of working at our organization along with the upside potential for continued progress. While times are bad now, we know that they will get better. There have been nine recessions since World War II and nine recoveries. I am betting that there will be a tenth. If we stay focused, aligned, and motivated on solving our customers' problems, we will be a much stronger company as we enter into the tenth recovery. And keep people loose. It is a turbulent economy; it is a depressed economy – it is not a children's hospital. Finally, don't fret about the things you cannot control. I cannot control what the NASDAQ did today. I cannot control whether or not there is war against Iraq. But what we can control is our own attitude about solving our customers' problems and staying focused on the mission of seeing the corporate world employ our solutions.

Looking forward, I foresee a tremendous amount of consolidation in the industry. There is $90 billion in the venture capital pipeline right now. There are somewhere on the order of 8,000 software companies. The world does not need all that money going to all those companies. There won't be nearly as many companies or nearly as much capital needed to start and raise companies, and I think that the requirements for growing a company will be much more stringent than they have been for our industry's short history.

In positioning a company for change, the motto is "Change or die." If you cannot change, you are by definition moving backward. The fact is that we live in fluid markets with customers who have new requirements and with employees who are faced with different paradoxes, priorities, and dilemmas on a daily basis. You have to keep your employees comfortable with change. You essentially have to do it from the top – by constantly changing yourself and how you are doing your job and how

42

you are working so that your message doesn't become stale, your organization doesn't become stale, and your product doesn't become stale. Resistance to change is futile because change will come with or without you.

We look at the future from the perspective of analyzing our strengths and our weaknesses. We analyze our opportunities, our threats, and the core competencies that we have and the core competencies that we need in the future. We look at the strategic challenges and/or changes that we must face and determine which initiatives will support getting them done right. Then we fill in the tactics and the finances to support all of that.

Advice for Small Businesses

Remember that everything will take longer than you expect and plan accordingly. Plan from a standpoint of scarcity, not abundance. Don't build in anticipation of revenue; build in reaction to revenue. Finally, do everything you can to make your revenue recurring or repeatable, so that people pay for your solution as they use it, not on a forward-looking basis.

It is important to recognize those who are interested in the basis of your value proposition and spend as much time as you can, focusing on their needs. Most importantly, recognize those people who really aren't interested and do not waste your time. Many entrepreneurs waste their time with prospects that really aren't that interested but, because they have a big title from a big company, the entrepreneurs spend too much time trying to convince them to care. Don't waste your time with suspects, tolerate prospects, and love your customers.

INSIDE THE MINDS

Finally, remember the golden rules of entrepreneurship:

Success will come through others, not you.
Everything takes longer than you expect because you are an optimist –
otherwise you would not be doing this.
Get rid of all the jerks in your organization.
Make sure you are solving a real problem – in this environment no one is
going to pay you for a bright idea.
Find out what people want and help them get it – they will always help
you get what you want.

Future entrepreneurial endeavors will be based around solving known business problems, and reducing the costs and time required to do business. The days of companies founded (and funded) simply on the basis of a promising technology, without a real market need, are over.

Bob Brennan joined Connected Corporation in April 2000 as the company's President and CEO. Previously, Brennan was employed with Cisco Systems as General Manager of Broadband Access Solutions, a software group focused on creating directory services for cable Internet access providers. Brennan also served as CEO of American Internet prior to its acquisition by Cisco in 1998. From 1993 to 1995, Brennan was the Vice President, General Manager for Merisel, a distributor of software and microcomputer products. While at Merisel, Brennan led 350 employees in 9 divisions and was responsible for $3 billion in yearly revenue.

As part of his leadership role at Connected, Brennan frequently advises corporations on how to best protect and secure their data, and establish best practices in PC information management. Recently, Mr. Brennan participated in "Building America's Information Shield," a broadcast discussion with government officials focusing on existing security and

BUILDING YOUR COMPANY

protection technologies, and the extraordinary steps the federal government and private industry are taking to insure critical systems are protected. Mr. Brennan has also been invited to comment on data protection and disaster recovery measures as part of several radio and television news programs, and for stories in national business magazines and technology-focused publications. Brennan received a BA in Psychology from Manhattan College.

Where to Begin

David Carlson
Synhrgy HR Technologies
Chairman, CEO & Co-Founder

Why Did I Start a Company?

There are many factors that contribute to a decision to start a company. In my case, I worked for a large organization; I saw the market heading in a certain direction, but the company was unwilling to move to take advantage of that trend (and, in fact, disagreed that it was a trend). So I left and started my own company. I left for a variety of reasons – vision and passion for one – I felt that the company I worked for was going to miss a big market. There was also the typical entrepreneurial frustration of working in a large company and having some restrictions on me that didn't feel comfortable.

So it was a combination of a passion and vision for where I thought the market was going, a bit of opportunistic belief that I could go out and build that business and succeed, and then my own interest in being in a situation in which I did not have so many restrictions around what I pursued. So my situation was probably very typical in terms of why somebody leaves a large company and a secure job for entrepreneurialism.

First and foremost, to succeed as an entrepreneur, you must have a vision and real passion around what you're doing. You have to believe very strongly that what you're doing is doable, that the market needs it, and that it's going to happen and you can help make it happen. It's very important to do something that you have a passion about – life is fairly short, and happiness and success in life means being around people you enjoy being around – but I also think you need to have a passion about what you do each day. A humorist said, "Find a job you like and you'll never have to work again"; now I don't feel that way always – some days it feels like work – but I have a hard time picturing myself performing in a role where I don't have passion. How unfortunate that would feel to me, to be working on something I have no passion about. Find something you like doing, and you will be successful at it. If you find something that you perceive as being successful but you don't like doing it, you won't be a success at it. You'll have to force yourself to get up every day and do your job.

You're an evangelist in the early years. And that's why the vision and passion are critical, along with trust. If you do not believe what you're saying, people will sense that, and they won't be interested in following you. The basis for following someone's vision is trust. When you say something you mean it, and when you're selling vision, trust is critical. Plus, the road to growing a company and being successful has a lot of hurdles, and each time you hit a hurdle, if you don't believe in the vision and have a passion about it and are trusted, it would be very easy for employees and other stakeholders to bail out.

Second, you have to find and recruit the most talented people in your industry, because the odds are against your success, and the better the people you have, the better your chance of making it. I suspect that if you studied entrepreneurial firms that have grown beyond their roots into successful growing companies, that someone in leadership felt very strongly about recruiting the best people possible. That person or persons in leadership was secure enough to hire people that may be better, smarter, harder working, etc., and the end goal of the organization was more important than the affect on the leader. Beyond the initial need for vision and passion, I believe this is the biggest reason some organizations stay small and some grow. The ones that stay small often have a leader or leaders that are uncomfortable not being the star in the organization, so they unconsciously seek out people who are not as strong or stronger than they are. Or if they find strong people, they manage them too tightly and drive them away.

When I say most talented in your industry, it's more than the technical depth, competencies, and the energy of the people; you also have to make sure you're selecting people who are comfortable in an entrepreneurial environment. An entrepreneurial environment is very different from a large corporation. You don't have nearly the time or resources to assess risks. There's much more intuition in the early years. You have to have a management team that has a deep knowledge of the industry, and, yet at the same time, they have to be comfortable in an entrepreneurial environment where risk is a big factor. We have hired very talented people from our industry who are uncomfortable and not successful in an entrepreneurial environment. The two reasons seem to be a discomfort with risk (risk paralyzes their decision making) and an unwillingness to do the tough tasks to push the organization along. You might use the phrase "Everyone carries their own water." You don't have a staff of people around you to study something or to write something; you do those things yourself. And the people who like that environment, where there's less structure and the reward-risk spectrum is different, thrive in it. The people who are uncomfortable with risk tend not to do well in it. So the third key is that you have to find people who are really comfortable in the ambiguity of an entrepreneurial company, because there's more risk, there's less known, and there's less structure. You have to find people who actually thrive in that environment, because those are the ones who keep the organization going.

Fourth, communicate a lot and continually remind everyone about the mission and vision of the company. This is particularly true in difficult times. In the absence of information, people generally assume the worst. And if you are the keeper of the vision, they need to hear why the vision is still valid, and why your organization will fulfill the vision in spite of evidence to the contrary. The talented people that joined you often have many opportunities available to them and in the day to day tasks they perform, it's easy to lose sight of the vision. A saying from ancient writings that is still true today is "Without a vision, the people will perish". So communication and keeping the vision in front of people can have a dramatic affect on long-term results.

WHERE TO BEGIN

Fifth, you have to be a jack of all trades and comfortable doing everything from the high-end tasks like strategy to the less sophisticated tasks like answering the phone. In the early years, you are a salesman, marketer, people manager, bookkeeper, etc. And as a company, you have to provide high-quality client work, you have to provide a lower cost than your competitors, you have to provide a service or product that is as good or better. Otherwise, you are always the second or third choice. A best-selling business book said that organizations tend to specialize in one of three areas – operational excellence, innovation, or client management. In the early years of an organization, you have to be good at all three. Maybe over time, one of the specializations will emerge as your greater strength, but in the meantime, you need to do all of them well.

Sixth, be careful whom you choose as your business partners. In terms of the external support team – whether that's legal counsel, bankers, strategic alliances, technology partners – it's critical that you not only can help each other but that you're culturally similar, that there's a high level of trust, and that you have a similar vision of where the business can go. If those things aren't there, those relationships get off track very quickly. I think there's a tendency when you're starting an organization (especially when you're in an industry that's capital-intensive like ours) to think that you need to partner with somebody much larger. And while that may end up being the right strategy, I would say for us as an organization, we rushed into a few marriages, so to speak, that should have been dating relationships – relationships that ended up not being worth our time and effort. If you do an alliance/partnership with someone, the cultural fit is as important as the deal itself. We learned that the hard way a few times, but our mistakes led us to better decision making around partnerships.

Finally, when you make a mistake as an organization – we certainly have made our share – you have to fix it quickly and move on. You don't have

INSIDE THE MINDS

the luxury that a big corporation has to put a lot of resources around it and spend a lot of time figuring out what went wrong and why. I think the "blame game" is the most destructive aspect of managing mistakes. I believe that people do things with the right intent and when a mistake is made, it's not an issue of intent, but rather the person's experience, judgement, not having enough data, etc. And it can be demoralizing to a group or an individual to question intent. The basic assumption should be that everyone is trying to do what they believe is best for their group/team/organization. That's a very different message and creates a very different culture than focusing on blame and questioning intent. At the same time, as an organization, you need to talk through what worked and didn't work and why the mistake occurred. In addition to not blaming people, it's critical to force the organization to focus on what was learned as opposed to what was lost. This keeps the entire organization moving forward and still willing to take calculated risks. My experience is that the culture in most large organizations is risk-averse because they focus on blame and who was at fault when something happens. They are so afraid of making a mistake that they eliminate all risk from the equation – and in doing so, they dampen the risk-taking entrepreneurial spirit in their people. The challenge for organizations like ours is to keep an innovative/risk oriented approach, even as we grow larger.

Early Days And Surveys

In the early years, what we had was a group of very experienced people – myself and the other co-founders who probably each had twenty years already in this industry – and who already had a pretty strong intuitive sense of where the market was going and spent a lot of time listening to companies in the process. And so, while we never did anything formally around survey research, ours was the traditional process of having some good ideas, bouncing them off clients, evolving them, and turning them

52

into products and services. However, not using surveys to determine where the market was heading was a problem when we looked for our first round of venture capital. The VCs asked us where our market research was, and we said it was based on our experience and reading "between the lines" with clients. One of the challenges in creating a new product is that market research tends to focus on that which is already known. The analogy I think of is if I surveyed people in the 1800s and asked, "Would you be interested in driving in a metal carriage that didn't need horses?", they would probably say no. Obviously, that market research was ineffective, even though it accurately reflected what people thought at the time. These days we have a more structured process around what we invest in and what we don't invest in. On an annual basis, we spend a lot of time thinking through where we think the market is headed, and then we spend a lot of time talking about where we would want to invest next year – where do we want to spend capital relative to that market? And while it's a more structured approach, there's still a certain amount of flexibility built into it, because our market is very dynamic right now. We could set a five-year plan, but frankly, the market will shift and move some. So we tend to look at things a couple of years out, but always recognizing that there's an element of flexibility in it, that we have to be prepared to shift gears fairly quickly.

A Business Plan

This is an area we still laugh about when we think back to the early years. We didn't write our first business plan until we went out for venture capital money. Of course, when you're trying to raise venture capital, a business plan is absolutely critical, because you're explaining to people who don't have the same experience in that industry where you think it's going, why you think it's going that way, and how you can create a business and make money at it. You cannot do that without a well thought-out business plan. And if the business plan is done right, it becomes an evolving living document.

Networking

To get a business going, there are two levels of network. The first level network was for myself and the other co-founders to individually use our own networks to present and propose opportunities, whether that involved a client or a strategic partner. There's no doubt that having a relationship – and certainly trust is part of that relationship – ahead of time is critical when you're a start-up, or people won't be interested in talking to you about something that they don't think you ought to be doing because you're so small. There are many people who start companies with a very detailed plan – they've raised money ahead of time and have the management team in place. That's not how we did it. Next time around I probably would do it more that way, but I certainly learned a lot in the process. The second level of networking is to find the people who can push the business along and who will be comfortable with the level of risk. Once you do that, then that group of people starts leveraging their relationships, both from a sales side and from a product development and operations side.

The hardest customer to win is definitely the first one; there's no question about it. A client that hires you – if they're the first client for something like our business – there's definitely a leap of faith on their part. I have warm thoughts about our first client to this day because I know they took a risk with us. It turned out to be good for them, but they took a risk.

Management Style and Focus

I don't think any particular style is right or wrong for being an entrepreneur. I know many entrepreneurs and their communication and management style vary widely. The perception is that entrepreneurs are driven people, never satisfied, temperamental, etc. While I'm driven to see Synhrgy be very successful, my communication style is not telling/demanding, etc. I come across more as a listener. My style works for me, but I don't think it would work for everyone. The more important aspect of management is the environment you create. I believe that if given the right environment, people will almost always do more than you thought they could, so the job of manager is to help to create the right environment. That includes some of the tactical things such as compensation programs and rewards, but it's also the cultural things around participative management – making sure people have some say in any decisions that are made that affect them. It takes more time to do that – you have to have more discussions and communication – but my sense is that when it's done right, the productivity in the organization is much higher than when people feel they're being forced to do something that they either disagree with or don't understand.

Now the reality is, when you do participative management, not everybody agrees with the outcome in the end, but at least they understand the process that got to the outcome. If they're going to be successful in business, at some point, if the majority says, "This is what we should do," or the leader says that they agree and dig in, even if they didn't agree with the decision – but at least they understand it.

As I said earlier, it's unusual for somebody to do something wrong intentionally. When people or groups make mistakes, it's usually because they don't have enough data, or haven't been in the process, or just lack experience in business. So I tend to say this often: "We're not here to question intent; we're trying to deal with how to solve this issue." And I think trust begets trust. I think the natural state of most people is to want to be trusted, and if you create an environment where people are trusted, it actually feeds on itself in a positive way. I think that's true with client relationships; I think that's true with any relationship. I have a trusting style and a style where I'm always trying to solve the issue as opposed to win it for my side.

My Evolving Role

In the early years, because we were very small, I did a bit of everything, and, at the same time, tried to keep the vision and the strategy going. These days, my job is evolving more into vision and strategy. The size that we've grown and the talent we've brought on in the last couple of years allows me to start to focus on the vision and strategy and strategic relationships. A CEO once said in a TV interview that the most important job of a CEO is to think deeply about the business they're in. And I would actually add to that: the leadership role, the cultural tone, the style, and everything that you set within the organization is the other extremely critical role.

If you're in a leadership role in an entrepreneurial organization, people look to you to react to everything, from good news to bad news. So you have a significant influence, especially in the earlier years, on how people feel about the company itself. Especially in the early years of an organization, when there are many roadblocks and hurdles, you have to keep reminding people of why you're doing what you're doing, how good the outcome will be some day, and that the market really is headed this way, even though it may not appear obvious. You have to spend a decent amount of time making sure everyone else feels the same passion, because it's easy to get off course, and when things get rough, if people lose the vision, they end up leaving. So I spend a lot of time with some of our talented younger managers in one-on-one conversations, just getting them enthusiastic about all the potential for this business because I know in the day-to-day trenches – focusing on working things out and solving problems – it's easy to lose the vision.

Attracting People

As I said earlier, you not only need to find top talent in your industry, but they also must be successful in the less structured entrepreneurial environment. We have had well over a 90 percent job acceptance rate, even when pulling people from more secure roles. The attraction gets back to the mission, vision, and a sense of purpose in building something like a company. People find it irresistible. But even if they find it irresistible, I use a simple tactical way to evaluate someone's fit in our environment. I ask them, as I describe this new large market and us as an emerging company in this market, "Does it get you more excited than scared, or more scared than excited? If you're more scared than excited, this is probably not the place for you. Because you're going to experience both emotions. If you're more excited than scared, this is probably the right kind of company."

So the reality is, any time someone is going to take a jump into an entrepreneurial firm that is not established, there's an element of excitement and an element of fear in everybody, and the ones who have a lot more fear than excitement probably shouldn't do it, because it's a bumpy road starting a company. In our case, we were out developing something that the market (both clients and competitors) didn't understand and wasn't ready to even accept that this was what they wanted to do. We entered a capital-intensive business where our smallest competitors have thirty times our revenue. We're a small entity selling to Fortune 500 clients, competing against huge companies – so if you're risk-averse, I think you'd find this place very anxiety-producing, especially in the early years.

INSIDE THE MINDS

These days, for senior roles, we look for people who have operated in both places successfully, because there are many people in an entrepreneurial environment you couldn't move to a corporate environment. It goes both ways. As we get larger, we start functioning more like a corporation; we do need more structure, and we do need to analyze risk more, so the type of people we've brought in the last year or so are generally those who have worked in both a corporate and an entrepreneurial environment and have been successful in both.

Managing During Changing Times

There is no doubt that in the last couple of years companies have developed a greater consciousness of cost. Given the turbulent economy, the projections that companies used to make about what they were going to sell or deliver have come way down, and there's a much more realistic view. This is true for us as well; we have a very realistic view of what our cost structure needs to be to meet good growth, as opposed to something that we hope happens that's way beyond that. So, first of all, there's a lot more discipline about what to spend money on in a turbulent economy.

Second, clients themselves are much more focused on saving hard dollars so our story has changed somewhat and while value is still critical, there must be a hard dollar Return-On-Investment for a company to invest in a change. Our product plays very well as a hard dollar investment, so that has become a bigger sales theme. While it was always there, it's now the first thing that comes out of our mouths: We can save you money!

Third, as I said before, in turbulent times you have to communicate more with employees, clients and other stakeholders. In tough times there's a lot of anxiety about job security in particular. There has to be more time

58

WHERE TO BEGIN

spent saying, "Hey, we're OK in spite of the economy, in spite of reading about layoffs at other companies. We're doing fine; there's no hidden message here." Mission, vision, and trust are critical here for people to accept the message that we're doing well in spite of the economy. Unfortunately, the people that can leave easily during difficult times are usually the best performers so it's critical to stay close to that group.

Trends

Our market is very dynamic right now. While many trends are affecting our industry, there is a confluence of three major trends occurring that all impact how human resources is delivered for large employers.

The acceptance of BPO as a viable business alternative
One significant trend that affects our firm is the broader trend in US and Global business to outsource and more specifically to outsource business processes. Business Process Outsourcing has been around for a while but in the last few years is gaining traction for large organizations. This includes some functions that are viewed as critical in a company but not necessarily critical to be delivered by the company. This could be business process outsourcing (BPO) for manufacturing, finance and accounting, or for human resources, which is our industry. Our original mission and vision was that organizations were going to outsource the majority of human resource (HR) business functions to organizations like us who can invest in technology, people, and processes but do it across many clients, driving down the costs and improving the value. We now have meaningful case studies of clients that have seen dramatic improvement in employee and manager satisfaction and have driven down the hard dollar cost of delivering human resource services. While we are excited that organizations are seeing the value of HR outsourcing, it also means that more players are entering the market and the competitors are actually getting larger and larger, and the smaller ones –

59

with the exception of us and probably one other – have disappeared. The smaller ones have either been bought or they've gone out of business.

So the trend towards BPO is an advantage to our business model, but it also means a changing competitive landscape that we need to continually address. Lastly, with the downturn in the economy, there is a greater focus on companies cutting cost, and business process outsourcing does that in certain models; it certainly does it in our model. So there has been a lot of change in our market, in terms of the players, what the clients are looking for, and, of course, as we grow, what we offer each year, too.

Technology and the proliferation of the web
While much has been written about this in the last five years, employee web use in the employer market is beginning to take off. Our client base comprises about 50 clients averaging about 15,000 employees each. This group runs the gamut of industries (manufacturing, service, high tech, etc.) and is seeing about 75 percent of their employees access HR services through the web. A year ago it was 55 percent and the year before that it was 35 percent. That's a very dramatic rise in usage. In addition, we are seeing 30 percent of the users access the web away from work so home access is increasing rapidly. (My sense is that this will be a requirement in the future for student research so most homes will have access regardless of the socioeconomic status of the household.) We also see about 30 percent of the access to the web occur after work hours or on the weekend. Again, quite a change from a few years ago. And we are also seeing retiree access to the web increase, although still around 20 percent today. (My mother, who is retired, keeps track of all of her friends through web email.)

The dotcom bubble burst seemed to imply that the web would not be as significant in our daily lives as the visionaries said it would a few years earlier. The early visionaries probably overstated the influence (e.g. solve world hunger), but now the market seems to be understating the influence. It still is the most effective and cost efficient way to deliver massive amounts of information but do so in a tailored way to each user. Some of the increasing web usage we are seeing is due to more sophisticated web products and also the greater acceptance and comfort in the US with using the web. We find that when we roll out a new web application for a client, the call volumes do not decrease in the first four or five months while web usage is still high. People tend to use the web and then call our service center to make sure it worked. But after that "comfort" period, call volumes drop.

The next wave of web technology in our business is moving more sophisticated transactions and decision support to the web for both managers and employees. This will be modeling on healthcare choices, career and development options, financial planning and retirement planning, and, for the manager, everything from compensation and performance planning for employees to strategic planning for senior management. These issues are as significant as an ability to measure the value of your people and the impact the culture and other programs have on financial performance.

The Last Trend - The Next Frontier in Business

In looking toward the future, I think the next frontier in business management is creating greater value through human resources or human capital or people – whichever term you prefer. And it's creating a culture and an environment that yields higher benefit from the employees. The story I always tell is, if I went to a refinery here in Houston, they could tell me within a drop of oil how that plant has performed for the last ten years. They could give me statistics on how that plant performed relative to other plants and what were the attributes of the plant. They could tell me in great detail how that capital asset has performed historically and it's contribution financially to the company.

But if I ask the same organization to tell me about the performance of their people or their human capital, they'd look at me with a blank stare. They couldn't tell me about the core competencies of the firm, the traits, skill sets, and tendencies of their senior executive staff, how they compare to other organizations in their industry and outside, or how the various human resource programs and policies affect the organization financially and managers and employees individually. And it's ironic because I personally believe people are the ultimate differentiator in a company. This is particularly true in organizations with a heavy concentration of knowledge workers and less capital assets, although I think it is true in both places.

I believe, executive management in the United States is starting to recognize this, but the strategy, systems, processes, and programs still employed at most large organizations do not lead an organization to drive greater value from their people. Or stated a better way, organizations limit the value that their people can add to the organization. Most organizations would say that the human resource department in their organization is there to help management create greater value from their people. The reality is most HR organizations have become administrative entities supporting the corporate programs but not driving the value of human capital. Today, the human resource department for a typical Fortune 500 company spends more than 70 percent of their time on administrative tasks. If you ask the CEO where the real value creation is for HR, it is not in doing administrative tasks. It is in creating the right culture and environment, getting the right people in the right job, at the right time, with the right reward system. I personally believe that an organization can improve organizational performance by at least 20 percent with an effective HR department. That can translate into significant Return on Investment and affect on financial performance. Unfortunately, the complexity of programs, the law, etc., has created this administratively focused HR department.

WHERE TO BEGIN

So how does a company fix this? Number one is to re-establish the purpose of HR and communicate that to the entire organization. This needs to be led by the CEO himself. "Our human resource department exists to provide consulting, information, and tools around culture, environment, performance, compensation, other policies, etc., to drive measurable value to the organization." Each constituent of the HR department needs to understand how HR will assist them with their company and individual goals, whether that is the executive management group looking at workforce analytics, business managers managing employee performance, or employees managing their own development.

The second step is to reorganize how the existing HR work is done. The administrative tasks can't be eliminated entirely, but they can be outsourced, moved to self-service, and largely taken out of the organization. This leaves a group of people in HR that are responsible for overall strategy, program management, vendor management, and business integration. This is a much smaller group than the original department with, on average, a more senior staff. And, in fact, this is why most people choose the HR profession – to work with people and managers and to create more value, not to fill out forms.

The third step is to determine how the HR department and the people of the organization will be measured on an ongoing basis. Without the ongoing measurement and continuous review of value, HR can often revert back to an administrative function. Today, the reengineered solution is allowing employers to have access to much more data about programs, policies, and their affect on the organization. We worked with one organization that could reduce hard dollar costs each year by about $50,000,000 across a 100,000 life workforce by more effective absence management. Some of it was the application of technology, new processes, and some outsourcing, but a lot of it was freeing up the HR staff so that they could focus on the value of the programs and in this case, the absence programs. Instead of HR spending all of its time on

63

INSIDE THE MINDS

administration, they could focus on innovative ways to create more efficiencies in the absence function.

Better program management in HR can have a significant hard dollar ROI and is critical to an organization creating more value from HR and their people. The next evolution of measurement (and not many companies are doing this today because the tools aren't quite there yet) is determining the value of your people and their contribution to the overall financial goals of a company. Questions like: What is our culture? Does our culture contribute to our mission, vision, and goals of the firm, of the department, of the team, etc.? If it contributes, does it do so at a greater level than our competitors? Does our management approach and philosophy contribute to our success? Do the organizations core competencies match well with the businesses we are in or want to be in? Does our leadership have the appropriate skills, strengths, etc., to lead us on our journey? What are the competencies of our top leadership team?

For employees, the issues can be: Am I in a role that matches well with my competencies, strengths, interests? Is there another role within the firm that is a better match – i.e. I can contribute more? If I want to develop into a supervisor, what skills and competencies do I need before I can be promoted? Today, the answers to the majority of these questions are not available from the HR department and if they are, it tends to be a very long and expensive consulting process to determine the answer. This new model using company experts, business process outsourcing, and technology for self-service will make these answers much quicker and affordable for everyone in the organization and will lead to a more successful organization.

Dave Carlson, Chairman, CEO and Co-founder of Synhrgy HR Technologies, Inc., drives the vision, thought leadership and strategic initiatives behind the company's innovative HR solutions. With 20 years of experience in the human resources industry, Carlson has acquired a broad and in-depth knowledge of the HR industry with expertise in business process outsourcing for benefit programs, human resource programs and information systems implementation.

Prior to co-founding Synhrgy, Carlson served as Principal and Director of outsourcing at Hewitt Associates, where he led the development and operation of a national service center in Houston. He received his Bachelor of Science degree in Business from Taylor University, and a Masters degree in Management and Management Information Systems from Northwestern University.

All the Right Ingredients

Bob Carr
Heartland Payment Systems
Founder, Chairman & CEO

Starting a Company

Many small businesses can compete effectively with large companies. Many large companies lose touch with their customers and their employees, the people who create the real value for those customers. Many large competitors are focused on gaining inexpensive marginal growth. Many competitors aren't willing to spend money to fix things that don't work or are inefficient. Or are they just too dumb to know the difference? All large competitors spend a lot of time, money, and energy on activities completely removed from adding value for their customers and for the workers who do the heavy lifting. These inefficiencies and this lack of proper focus create opportunities for small companies to peck away at the revenue growth of larger competitors. If you understand this for your industry as well as you understand anything, you may be ready to start your company.

Why start a company? Start a company because you want to take responsibility for your career in the ultimate way. You will be directly at fault for the mistakes and will be able to take much of the credit for the successes. You will have no shackles to hold you back, but you will also have no safety net to catch you when you fall. Start a company because you can no longer tolerate roadblocks placed in your way by those with contrary personal agendas or the inability to see the truth as you see it. Start a company because you believe you know how to do things better than anyone else has ever done them. Start a company because you want to create opportunities for your employees and partners. Start a company because you feel that you can make a contribution by making this a better world with a new paradigm. Start a company because you just can't be happy marching to the beat of someone else's drummer.

I started my business because I felt that others were doing many things wrong. More importantly, I believed that I knew how to do them correctly right from the start. I knew exactly what was needed to get a strong start. I thought I knew the recipe for success and so I found or developed each of the necessary ingredients before starting. Before baking a cake, you first make certain that you have each of the ingredients and kitchen tools at your disposal. It's the same in starting your business. You need:

The Right Stuff

To get a business off the ground successfully, you must know all of the required ingredients and in what proportions you will need them. That includes the tools you will need to mix the ingredients and cook the batter. And you better have lots of experience baking cakes for others with someone else's ingredients and recipe before you start to use your own resources. If you haven't done something similar to your business idea before, you should learn how to do it before starting your business. On-the-job training when you start your own business can be hazardous to your enterprise. If you don't know what you don't know or how to learn or where to look for information, you need more experience on the job and more work after hours before jumping into the fire.

I started Heartland Payment Systems after twenty-five years of working as a small guy with big ideas and no resources. When significant resources finally became available to me at a reasonable cost, I knew how to use them and avoided making big mistakes. In the ten years before Heartland, my tiny business built a merchant portfolio of $500,000,000. My partners and I found a willing partner with something none of us had ever had before – real capital. We contributed our business and our new partner contributed $1,000,000. We took that capital and our recipes and started our new company. Thirty-eight months later we bought out our partner for $15,000,000 in cash. A year later, we sold that interest to new partners for $40,000,000. We built a very big company. In five years, we grew to be twenty-four times larger and were ranked by INC Magazine as the 57th fastest growing private company in the US.

Happy, Profitable Customers

We had the benefit of ten years of experience operating on a shoe string (much too long) and learned tons from past mistakes, large and small. One thing we knew how to do was to find customers and make them happy while making a reasonable profit. Learning how to do that was priceless. It is tough to get started in a new business if you don't know exactly how to find your customers. If you don't already have your first clients lined up and if you don't have a key sales person who will land these first clients for sure, you aren't ready to start your business.

In addition to knowing how to find your customers, you must know how to make them happy and how to make a reasonable profit at the same time. If you can find a few customers, make them happy, and make a reasonable profit, you will be able to do it on a larger scale if you can find, recruit, motivate, reward, and teach others how to do what you have done. Creating happy customers and earning a reasonable profit is the first goal.

You won't know that things are getting off the ground successfully until you have objective feedback from the marketplace. The objective marketplace will tell you if you are selling the product/service you had envisioned at the price and margin you forecasted in your initial plan (or a revision to that plan), delivering the service at a quality level acceptable to the marketplace, and generating enough business to reach the breakeven point. You need to know that you can make customers happy while creating a profit. Next, if you want to get big, you need to build a team of believers.

To succeed at these crucial steps you must be a leader. Doing everything yourself is OK, but it does not necessarily make for a good business. You must develop team members who will follow your dream. How can you have confidence in your plan or your leadership ability if there is nary a soul who is willing to follow you? If you don't have people ready to buy into your dream, you should wait because you are not ready. To be a successful businessperson you need to know how to create successful relationships with both customers and employees who will benefit long-term from your business execution.

Risks Worth Taking

Why start a business? If you are unhappy in your present career, you should be willing to risk a lot to gain the ability to be happy building something you can be proud of. If you aren't willing to risk a comfortable lifestyle, then you will need to jump in the water with OPM (other people's money) from the start. You will need the support of your family if you are giving up a secure income to make the jump. This is all part of the planning process. You must make hard decisions if your family does not support your desire to start a business. It is difficult for anyone to trade the security of a happy family life for a plunge into waters unknown. Make sure you are absolutely honest with your family about the risks, and if they support you, you are a fortunate person. These are life-changing decisions that can go either way.

Entrepreneurs are special (or is the proper word "crazy"?) because they are willing to take the risks of failure and to put their ideas on the line in an objective marketplace. Lots of smart folks talk about becoming entrepreneurs but are mostly talk, talk, talk and full of all kinds of ideas and advice. It is a rare individual who has enough self-confidence and moxie to trust the marketplace to keep score. Are you really an entrepreneur or do you just like to talk about the theory?

When taking risks, there will be problems and steps backward. If I could do it all over again, I would have sought more advice and gained more experience before I left my comfortable career. I would have worked harder to find someone who had done what I wanted to do. The fact is, I didn't know where to look to find such a person. I should have tried harder because there are hundreds of very successful people in virtually every field of endeavor. I paid a heavy price to go off on my own, and I wandered in the darkness of the woods and underbrush for a very long time. But I never regretted doing what I did for more than a few days at a time. Taking real risks with your career is something you have to experience to understand. To say that it is a gut check is an understatement.

Proof of Concept

The biggest stumbling block in starting a new business is defining a scaled down version of the initial business plan that allows for "proof of concept" without starving the entrepreneur and her family. Too many considering entrepreneurship spend a lot of time trying to offload all of the risk of their plans, ideas, and dreams to others - investors. The biggest stumbling block while starting your own business is being able to think small enough to prove the value of the plan in the real world. Many egos are too large to allow for this possibility.

It is difficult to start a successful business without both initial and longer-term written goals and plans. Lay out the plan in advance and make corrections as you go. Many people love to talk and analyze, but too much talk and analysis will drag you down. Establish goals - daily, weekly, monthly, quarterly, or annually, but don't get too carried away. Execution is the part that creates revenue and builds the platform for success. The most important goal is to create the value and cash flow you

ALL THE RIGHT INGREDIENTS

had originally forecasted as quickly as possible. Prove your concept in the real world as much as you can as quickly as possible.

When creating the initial business plan, intellectual honesty is the most important ingredient. The next most important is to develop a plan that can work on a small scale very quickly with the least amount of outside money and outside "management talent." You should try to prove your concept before reaching out for financing. Other smart people may view this differently than I do. OPM in the very beginning stages has a very huge cost and brings loads of baggage with it.

It is much, much better to prove your business model with your own resources, if possible. If it is not possible, then initial funding with OPM may or may not be better than waiting to build your own savings account. You should strive for initial success, giving up as little of your future upside as possible. Think very hard about this subject. Most entrepreneurs aren't too savvy about how those "other people" will view the value of their money when you have proven nothing but your quixotic enthusiasm and dedication to an unproven concept.

If your plan will work on a large scale, it will work on a small scale if you do most of the work yourself. If you prove your business model quickly in the real world, you will be able to negotiate for money and talent with much more credibility, and therefore be able to maximize your share of the business for what is important - the long run.

The Next Steps of the Planning Process

After you have proven your concept to yourself, it is time to move into the next stage of your plan. To get bigger, you will need more resources and more people to follow you. If you have created an effective business model, you will be able to convince new teammates of your vision.

It is crucial to set specific goals every step of the way for each person you add to your team. The more stakeholders that you make part of your business, the more understated your goals should be. Entrepreneurs should have huge goals. But these goals should be kept to yourself when recruiting your teammates and when soliciting investors. You should understate your goals to your potential stakeholders with a plan that you will most certainly outperform. Your knowledge, plan, and leadership will carry the day. Goals that appear to be extreme, even if realistic to you, will turn off almost every other serious person. Understate your true goals, but do everything you can to meet them after everyone is committed. You will become everyone's hero.

Do not rely too much on advisors who are not as expert as you. Consulting with accountants, lawyers, and mentors can be valuable to the process, but often these authority figures are used by fledgling entrepreneurs as a comfort cushion and can become a means to avoid getting down to business execution. You must have a written plan and you must be able to defend every word of it to yourself. If you believe in your plan and if you are an intellectually honest person, don't let advisors talk you out of your plan. You better know more about your business than they will ever know!

For me, success is measured by creating and providing a business model that succeeds for employees, customers and myself, as well as all of the other stakeholders. I want customers who love my company, and employees who want to work for my company for the rest of their careers because they will meet their personal goals by doing so.

Bring in the lawyers and accountants to help organize your corporate structure, but only after you have read up on the pluses and minuses of the alternatives. If you need to bring in lawyers for advice in how to do business, you don't have enough experience yet. Always bring in the lawyers to review important contracts before you sign them and always enter into written agreements with all contractors and vendors who are stakeholders in your success.

Obtaining Funds

Funding is the hardest part for many entrepreneurs. My biggest failure as a businessperson was not investing enough time to learn about funding a business in the right way. If I could do it all over again, I would have waited until I learned more about this subject. I was a "babe in the woods" and it has cost me hundreds of millions of dollars. Landing the funding is a major step, and it is also the beginning of the absolute requirement to perform. You get your company jumpstarted by achieving success in meeting your initial goals in the first weeks and months. If you can do what you thought you could do in the first weeks and months, you have a terrific start. (The converse is also true.) After you have proven your concept, you can effectively go out and raise funds to grow.

Knowing what I know now, after raising $41,000,000 of "growth capital," finding funds was the most difficult part for me. Those wishing to invest funds always have an agenda, and, oftentimes, that agenda is in direct conflict with that of the entrepreneur. No matter how smart your financial partners may think you are about your business, they invariably will think they know more about "money" than you do. After all, it's their money! It is their right. The need for money causes many entrepreneurs to make fundamental compromises to their business models, which often destroy the idea, the company, and the dreams. How desperate are you for growth? That is a very important question to ask before you seek funds from "other people".

The best way to bring in money is to have written goals and objectives for all parties. You should probably hire a professional to help you raise money. Most importantly, you must execute the business plan that

INSIDE THE MINDS

formed the foundation of the investment. Failure to execute the plan will always lead to a bad outcome for the entrepreneur. The investors will rightly do everything possible to cover their backside (with your head) and that is the way is must be whether we like it or not. Such is the price of OPM.

Getting Others Involved

As far as putting together the right team, you must have a solid plan, the leadership abilities to convince others of its importance, and the resources to compensate those who are investing their time and careers with you. Of course, finding these resources must be one of the fundamental parts of your plan. Each of the key people should be made a stakeholder in the success of the business. In order to be successful, team members need to believe that they are doing worthwhile work and being fairly treated and compensated for their efforts. They must believe they are on the best possible path for their career. Once a member of your team is on board, reward creative thinking and do not punish failures made with proper intent.

You must be able to get others around you excited and motivated about your business. This is the easy part. You have to genuinely believe in what you are doing and why you are doing it. You must have the resources to honor all of your commitments. If all of that is in place, then you need to make sure that your plan offers reasonable rewards for the people you are asking to place their faith in you.

Give your people resources, authority, a plan, and measurable goals. Then get out of their way and let them have the chance to succeed or fail without you looking over their shoulder too frequently. Remember how you wanted to be treated when you were working on someone else's agenda?

76

You need to show them how they can meet their dreams if they help you meet your dreams. You must nurture them, and you must reward and recognize them for outstanding performance. But above all of that, you need to treat them just like you would want to be treated by the people you thought "didn't get it."

The Role of Leadership

You must believe in what you are doing. Create a compelling value proposition and have real passion for making it all happen. Your genuine enthusiasm combined with expert knowledge will convert just about everyone (except potential investors who usually need more). Your leadership ability will allow you to network to find your teammates and allow your teammates to help you build the rest of your team and your client base. If you know what you are doing, you will be able to convince others to take advantage of the opportunity you are presenting. The more people you can convince, the more people they will convince. Lots of people are looking for something better. Your job is to make sure your business plan provides the income to compensate everyone as promised for the long haul.

As the founder of your company, you should have fundamental knowledge of all aspects of the business you want to start. To the extent you lack basic knowledge in an important area, you should have someone on your management team that you know well and have reason to trust. If your knowledge and expertise are lacking in fundamental areas, you may not be ready to start your business. Gaining knowledge is a continuous process, as you must always maintain your edge. Read all of the industry publications. Attend the trade shows. Get to know your competitors. Talk to customers and employees at every level and gain their trust so they always trust you enough to tell you the truth.

Your expertise, your business plan, your leadership abilities and your resources will dictate the size and depth of the management team you can or should hire. Each crucial person should be allowed to earn an ownership position in the company. The deeper and broader your management team, the more quickly you will meet your goals and objectives if you know what you are doing.

My management style (at least in theory) is to define the goals and objectives and to find the best person possible to do the job. We agree on the goals and objectives and the resources required. Then we define and agree upon the ground rules. Once we are in agreement on all of this, we decide how we will measure success and failure. At that point, I give that person the right and responsibility to use the defined resources to achieve the objectives he or she sees fit as long as he or she lives by the rules. We measure the successes and failures as agreed in advance.

We are all leaders. It is a question of what we are leading and where we are headed. The worst part about being a leader is the fear of leading people down a failed path. Another tough part is sorting out the real issues from the personal agendas of your employees. And then there are the real life problems of real people who are trying to fight their way through family and personal problems. Never, ever hire a person who lies to you. Always have all employee candidates complete an employment application, and terminate them if you later find that they lied in a material way – always! You get through these "people problems" by establishing the rules of engagement within your company and enforcing the rules fairly. But never accept dishonesty in your employees. If you do, you will have a dishonest business and it will be your fault!

Treat everyone as you want to be treated. Be more honest than you have to be. Tell the truth and be honest with yourself. Remember that intellectual honesty is the most important requirement for a successful entrepreneur with big ideas.

The Future

Our industry and the marketplace in general have changed considerably since we began. Our world is much more technology driven, and that opens up more opportunities all of the time. Also, our competition is run more and more by financial engineers who want to strip out as much expense as possible and charge the customer more for less. This is the perfect time to launch a business. A lot of people have made a lot of money and they aren't as hungry as those prepared to work like they have never worked before. Don't be intimidated by the prior successes of others. They have some of the ingredients you lack today, but your energy and willingness to sacrifice will carry the day for you. Your dreams can be attained, and in their attainment, you will have accomplished something that is very important.

Bob Carr is the Founder, CEO and Chairman of Heartland Payment Systems, the nation's largest privately owned merchant acquirer and ninth largest overall, with annual revenues exceeding $300,000,000. Heartland was recognized by INC Magazine as the 57th fastest growing private companies and one of the ten largest INC 500 companies. Bob was a Founder and Vice President from 1988 to 1990 of the Bankcard Services Association, which has since become the ETA.

Before entering the bankcard industry in 1986, he developed computer software systems for unattended fuel pumps and created the first integrated accounting applications for PCs. He also started the computer department at the Bank of Illinois and served as the Director of the Computer Center and as a mathematics instructor for Parkland College.

He earned degrees in mathematics and computer science from the University of Illinois in 1966 and 1967.

Inside Reality Versus Outside Perception

Richard C. Harshaw
MSI Marketing, Inc.
CEO

Inside Reality and Outside Perception

There are two basic concepts that a businessperson has to understand. One is the inside reality of their business, and the other is the outside perception of their business. The inside reality has to do with everything that that company does that makes it valuable to the marketplace. That could be the quality of its products or services, it could be a function of the systems that it has in place, or the customer service that it provides, or the people it has on staff – whatever it is that makes a company valuable to the market place is what we call the inside reality. There is a reality as to how valuable each and every company is based on its ability to serve the customer. The outside perception is how the prospects and customers of that business perceive it. That perception is formed based on the company's marketing communications, so if a company places an ad or has a website or has any kind of brochures or other marketing materials, those things are going to forge this outside perception.

This is the pitfall that almost no business owner really understands. Most business owners tend to be good at doing what they do. If someone has an auto repair shop he tends to be a good mechanic, if he's a financial planner he tends to be good at planning finances, but because he's not a communications expert, his ability to communicate his inside reality to the prospects and customers is virtually nonexistent. So based on what he says in his marketing and advertising, the customer or prospect never really gets an inkling or a clue as to what makes this company valuable.

Companies will typically use platitudes in their marketing and advertising efforts. A platitude is a statement or a word that is drearily commonplace, predictable, and, due to overuse or repetition, lacks power to evoke interest, but it is stated as though it is original or significant. This is what you find is most marketing and advertising. For example, let's say a moving company runs an ad in the yellow pages; that ad might say, "We do local and long-distance moves." Well, no kidding! What

INSIDE REALITY VERSUS OUTSIDE PERCEPTION

other kind of move is there? That doesn't tell you anything about what makes this company unique or special or good. They might continue in that yellow pages ad to say that they load and unload trucks. Well, no kidding! They might say that they service residential and commercial. They might say things like they're fully insured. But none of those things are anything but platitudes.

This is what you find in almost every single marketing and advertising piece on the face of planet Earth – platitudes. The company's inside reality (what they sweated and spent years and thousands and millions of dollars to create as a company) is not communicated at all to their customers and prospects, so the outside perception is simply, "Here's a company that's exactly the same as every other company." That's the worse position you can possibly be in.

To marry the inside reality to the outside perception, you have to use what we call the marketing equation. The marketing equation is a formula that allows you to match up the inside reality and the outside perception. The marketing equation is a four-step process: interrupt, engage, educate, and offer. To get someone to take action and buy something from you, you have to get the customer, the prospect, interrupted. You have to get him or her to take a look, and there are a couple of key concepts that are really critical in determining whether or not a company can get its prospect interrupted effectively or not. The problem with most advertising is that you're interrupting people based on things that are not important to them, so it doesn't have any impact. You have to break people out of their state of not paying attention; we call it alpha mode.

Typically people are in alpha mode. Alpha mode is simply the day-to-day habitual state of not thinking consciously about things. Have you ever driven to work and when you got there you realized you hadn't seen anything along the way because you were thinking of something else?

83

That's called alpha mode. Beta mode, on the other hand, is the active state of engagement where you're consciously processing and thinking about things. In marketing, we have to get somebody snapped out of alpha mode and into beta mode. That's obvious, but it's hard to do it effectively, and to do it effectively you have to understand one more concept, which is what we call the reticular activator. The reticular activator is the portion of your brain that is on the lookout twenty-four hours a day, seven days week, looking for things that are either familiar or unusual or problematic. For example, I bought a new green Ford Excursion last year and, after I bought it, guess what I noticed? Everybody on the face of the earth has the exact same color, make, and model of car, and the reason is that once you buy that car it now becomes familiar to you and your reticular activator has the ability to pick that out. It pokes your conscious brain on a subconscious level and says, "Hey, look – there's one just like yours." Your brain is always looking for these kinds of things that are, familiar, unusual, or problematic. What we like to do in marketing is to focus on things that are problematic. If we can communicate things that are problematic to a customer, then he'll identify with those problems because he experiences them and his reticular activator will poke his conscious brain; it will snap him out of alpha mode and into beta mode, and now he'll be engaged in our message.

Let's use moving again as an example. As mentioned earlier, most moving companies in their advertisements would put "We load and unload, we do commercial and residential, and we do local and long-distance" – all the usual kinds of platitudes that don't really communicate anything. Well, there are issues when it comes to moving that most customers don't know about. One of the major ones has to do with insurance coverage. There are three kinds of insurance when it comes to moving. One is called self-insurance, which is illegal and which means if you fine me and I happen to have money we'll pay for your broken stuff – about 5 percent of companies have that. The second

INSIDE REALITY VERSUS OUTSIDE PERCEPTION

is what they call "per-pound replacement insurance," meaning if you have a 25-inch TV and I break it as a mover, we'll pay you $.40 per pound to replace it; it weighed 40 pounds so we'll give you a check for $16.00 to replace your $300.00 television set. And then there's full replacement insurance, which means that you get a new TV if they break it, or whatever the case may be. Most companies don't offer full replacement insurance as a standard procedure; they offer per pound replacement insurance. So as we write our marketing and advertising materials, we're going to know that that's a potential hot button for the customer – something that needs to be pointed out to them.

In the marketing materials we will put a headline that says something about things that you don't know about moving, or something like "Here's how most moving companies can afford to charge you such a low price: They're making it up by not having the right kind of insurance, so that when your things get broken you get little or nothing." Remember, the reticular activator looks for things that are familiar, problematic, or unusual, so if we tap into this problematic hot button then it has the ability to get the person engaged in our ad, and it makes them look at our ad instead of the other 10 or 20 or 50 or 100 competitors because they're all saying the same usual platitudes. When we start talking about the actual problems consumers face, then they automatically, via the reticular activator, have no choice but to look at our ad and become engaged in it because we now promise them a solution to their problem, and people want to make the best decision possible at all times. Nobody ever went to a car dealership, negotiated a deal, and then took the third best deal they could get. Everybody wants to get the best deal. They want to make the best decision, but nobody ever had enough information to make the best decision because most companies are communicating platitudes instead of real information that is important to the consumer.

85

Now, if I am talking about insurance problems in the headline of my ad, am I communicating anything about my inside reality to the target market? Yes, I definitely am, because I'm talking about these issues, and I'm talking about how I solve those issues, and how I make sure that the customer doesn't get burned by those issues. My inside reality is that my company offers full replacement insurance as a standard practice. Yes, it may cost more, but you're going to be protected more. Now my inside reality and my outside perception start to match up, and they start to reflect the exact same thing, unlike with most companies. Most companies that have a good inside reality say things that are platitudes, so they appear on the surface level – on the advertising level, on the outside perception level – to be identical to companies that probably are a lot worse than they are. The consumer can't tell. The consumer can't pick that out. The consumer has no way to know. So when they look at the advertisements, when they start to search and decide whom to do business with, and everything appears to be equal, the customer will always default to asking how much it costs – because that's the only thing they know to ask because you have failed as a marketer.

So what does someone starting a business need to know about marketing? He needs to know that he has to get his inside reality up to snuff first of all. He has to have a business that's valuable, that's worthy of getting business, and once that's accomplished, he has to communicate in such a fashion that the inside reality becomes the outside perception. We do that with the marketing equation "interrupt and engage," based on the concepts we talked about: alpha and beta mode, reticular activator. Once we've engaged the prospect based on those headlines, based on those hot buttons, based on those issues that are important to get him out of alpha mode and into beta mode, then it becomes important to educate (step three of the marketing equation).

Now we move from an emotional cell to a logical cell. We got the prospect interrupted and engaged on the emotional level of the problem,

INSIDE REALITY VERSUS OUTSIDE PERCEPTION

and now we're going to logically show them how we solve those problems. We're going to set standards. We're going to show them what they need to look for. Again, in the case of our example of a moving company, we educate customers about what they need to know, what kind of issues are relevant and important, and we educate them as to those things.

Then there is the offer. This is the fourth step of the marketing equation. The offer, ironically, is typically for more information, because in an advertisement it is often difficult to give all of the educational information that the customer needs. So if we use this formula (interrupt, engage, educate, and offer), here's what we find. Results become inevitable because we're talking about things that the customer feels are important – things that will interrupt the prospect, things that will get them engaged – and then we're demonstrating by building a case and educating them as to how we do things and why we're superior and how things ought to be. Then for them to take action and do business with us is an inevitable end result.

A lack of understanding of marketing is the biggest stumbling block entrepreneurs face. If a company cannot understand how to get that outside perception matched up with its inside reality, it's going to be difficult. You've heard that old saying about if you build a better mousetrap it doesn't guarantee that the world is going to beat a path to your door; all that means is that a good inside reality does not guarantee a good outside perception. I think most businesses that fail do so not due to lack of good ideas, but due to a lack of good marketing and getting the message out there in an effectively communicated way.

87

INSIDE THE MINDS

Management Style and Vision

Some people think my management style is autocratic. A business owner ought to have a vision of what he wants to have done – a vision of what he's trying to accomplish – and he ought to put systems in place to allow himself to replicate his own abilities and his own thinking as much as possible. You're setting a lot of boundaries, a lot of limits. I would look at that and say, "I know what works, and I'm going to systematize the things that work so that people who come in who are not as full of vision as I am can still execute my plan."

The leader is the one with the vision. The leader is the one with the ability to see something that doesn't exist, to believe that it is true, and to make it come into reality. Leaders have the ability to get other people to see thier vision, to sell other people on that vision, to create the future today very clearly, very brightly, very full of color, and to have people get excited about that and execute their plan. The leader's number one job is to have the vision, to create that vision, to communicate that vision, and to really expand that vision so that everybody will grow.

This becomes a communication function: understanding the vision and communicating it. If you have an entrepreneur who does not have the ability to communicate that vision, then you essentially don't have an entrepreneur.

Having the right people on board is also a critical element. Hiring is a trial-and-error process for most entrepreneurs. My advice is to hire people for the job; don't just hire people who are good employees and then try to fit a job to them. One of the pitfalls of small businesses is hiring friends and family members. You need to identify the responsibilities and things that need to be accomplished, and then look for people who can fill those specific responsibilities and who have the

INSIDE REALITY VERSUS OUTSIDE PERCEPTION

necessary qualifications. If that happens to be a friend or family member, then great, but if not, be cautious.

So how do you get employees motivated? How do you get them to do things? There are many management techniques that can be employed – rewards and so on. I'm a big believer in the fact that what gets rewarded gets accomplished, but you have to communicate the vision of the company effectively and frequently to as many of the employees (and even vendors and partners) as possible, so that they stay excited about it.

Small businesses can execute a vision much better because larger companies start having too many people who are not personally attached to that vision, and they're executing someone else's vision – and by the law of diminishing returns, you're just not going to be able to execute that vision. That's why you see larger companies lose touch with their customers. They lose touch with what's important to the marketplace because people who don't have the vision are trying to execute the vision – and in many cases trying to create a vision – whereas in a smaller company, the vision is right there with the entrepreneur, and he has the ability to execute that and implement that on a very passionate person-to-person level, and it becomes a lot easier to execute. So many of the mobility issues of smaller companies have to do with the vision of the company and the ability of that vision to be seen and acted upon every day. You go to a large company, and you go to the 17th manager in the 13th district, and he doesn't have any idea what the vision of the company is. All he knows is that he's trying to collect his paycheck and not spill coffee on his trousers.

There's very little downside to being a leader. Of course, you have to catch all the flak and you have to deal with all of those who don't see the vision, but that is just part and parcel of the deal. I think how you deal with that just comes down to your own personal vision. If it is bright enough and secure enough and you believe it enough, there's really not a

INSIDE THE MINDS

lot that can bring you down off that vision. It's just not going to happen. Any non-truths or nay-sayers or complainers or issues that come up are completely non-issues because I know my vision's true. I know what it looks like. I know that we're on our way to it. So I don't really care what anybody has to say.

At the end of the day, if I can look at my productivity for the day on an enterprise-wide basis and on a personal level and say, "Today the vision has grown and today we have made quantifiable, measurable strides toward it," then that will keep me up late at night and get me up early in the morning – and keep me up mentally all day long.

To this end, I would ask this of all entrepreneurs and would-be entrepreneurs: What is your vision? In my opinion, if your vision does not include ruling the world within the sphere of what you do or what industry you're in, then you're not an entrepreneur. If your "vision" is to create a nice little business to pay you a half a million or a million dollars a year, or to create some jobs in the community, they you're not an entrepreneur. You're just a guy who doesn't work well having a job and wants to own his own job. On the other hand, if finding new and better ways to do things makes you tick, if the industry status quo disgusts you, if you prefer to fly in the face of traditional wisdom, and if creating the best company within your industry, and thereby hogging up all the market share to prove you're the best, motivates you, ah, now we have an entrepreneur. That's why the vision is so important. That's why it's all-important; it's the ONLY thing. It's the birth of that vision and the daily growth of it that keeps the entrepreneur going. It's knowing that you're the best at what you do, even though you don't have the time or the bandwidth presently to execute 95 percent of the vision you see. It's knowing that as soon as the competition catches up, you'll be four more steps ahead in executing your vision, and 127 steps ahead in expanding what you see and can create in your mind – this is what the true essence of entrepreneurship is all about. So I would ask one more time: What is your vision?

Richard C. Harshaw, CEO of MSI Marketing Inc., is one of the nation's leading marketing minds and business leaders. Even at an early age, he was starting businesses and making money. While in college, he learned how to speak Chinese and started an import-export business that sent all kinds of products in and out of Taiwan and China. He graduated from Brigham Young University with a degree in marketing and entrepreneurship.

Shortly after graduation, his domestic supplier of motor oil raised it's prices by 50 percent, and Rich was out of business. "That was a real blessing in disguise," says Rich, "I never would have gotten interested in marketing if I stayed in the export business. My first job after that was telemarketing. We were trained to use hard closes and stretch the truth. I quit after four days. If I stayed I would either starve from lack of sales, or go morally bankrupt from lying to people. I thought there's got to be a better way to sell than shoving it down people's throats."

Over the next 2 years, Rich read over 200 books on the subjects of business, marketing, sales, communication, motivation, and success. He started to formulate the ideas that would later become the foundation of the "Monopolize Your Marketplace" system. Rich then moved to Texas and took a job with a small office supply company as director of marketing to test his ideas. "It was like a little marketing laboratory to test out all my ideas and theories of what would motivate people to buy. We tried things that were totally unheard of in that industry and they worked." Six months later, Rich bought out the company, and then turned around and sold it 12 months after that for a nice profit.

By this time, Rich had teamed up with Edward Earle, an established

INSIDE THE MINDS

business builder, marketing consultant and seminar leader. "Edward had the ability to speak, and I had the ability to write all of the promotional materials and write letters and ads for clients. It was a perfect setup for both of us." Even in the early days of their partnership, they would consistently sell out seminars and have participants line up for their consulting services.

In the next several years, Rich became one of the nation's most sought-after business consultants because of his ability to write things in a way that motivates people to buy. He wrote ads and sales letters for top trainers like Brian Tracy and Dennis Waitley. He has written advertising and sales materials for all sizes and types of businesses, including the country's largest roofing company, Texas' largest SBA lending bank, the nation's largest provider of digital cellular service, and over 1,500 other companies. His articles about marketing, sales, and advertising have been seen in dozens of magazines and newspapers around the world.

Product Differentiation from Technology

Marina Hatsopoulos
Z Corporation
CEO

Getting the Business Off the Ground

The most important thing to focus on when starting a company is getting a product to market – defining the product, knowing who the customers are going to be, and having a product that satisfies a real need. That involves defining the market, defining the market size, and knowing that if you sell this product and it does satisfy a need, that you will be able to make money satisfying the need. You get your business off the ground by setting yourself apart and offering something that has some product differentiation and that satisfies a need. If you are unique and satisfy a need, that is power.

I think there are three skills that are very important in starting up a business. The first is being able to stay organized and prioritized in order to be comfortable juggling a lot of activities. There are a wide range of tasks that need to be done, and a start-up is typically under resourced, which means that the entrepreneur does everything from customer calls and patent filings to payroll and landlord relations. Some of these tasks are very important and some are urgent. There is always a tendency to put out fires and do the most urgent tasks first, whether or not they are the most important. It is important to keep the activities prioritized so that all the activities on the bottom of the list that do not get done (and there will always be an infinite supply of these), are the least important ones.

The second is being able to sell, because you are selling from day one. You are selling the vision, trying to hire good employees, selling the product, trying to raise money – whatever it is, the selling skills are extremely important to success.

The third skill is being able to negotiate. The company has one chance to be successful without running out of money, so it is important to negotiate everything effectively in order to preserve cash. Negotiating is

PRODUCT DIFFERENTIATION FROM TECHNOLOGY

important not just for money matters, but also (perhaps more so) for contractual matters: employment agreements, sales agreements, supplier agreements, joint development agreements, and confidentiality agreements. These are legal documents that the entrepreneur should become familiar with and understand so that negotiation can take place quickly and efficiently, ideally without requiring the lawyers to review every small change. This only makes sense if you know the relative importance of each of the issues so that you know when it makes business sense to give in.

A big resource early on, at least for us, was having a former life and knowing people with a lot of experience. We brought several people onto our board of directors, and we have used the board tremendously. Even outside of the board, it has been helpful just having contacts so that we can talk to people who have specific experience in a particular area and tap into that experience. It is amazing how a complex problem appears very simple after you speak with someone who has experience with that particular issue.

From the very beginning, you also need lawyers. They are critical for setting up the corporate structure, the stock, the equity structure, options, and also for protecting intellectual property (filing patents, trademarks and copyrights, and protecting know-how). I think they need to be involved from day one.

In the company's development, there are three stages and three different funding needs. There is the initial seed money just to set up operations; that amount will vary greatly, depending on what the business is. There is money to develop the product to get to the first sale, and that can be more or less, depending on how long that development is going to take and how capital intensive it is. The third step is getting to positive cash flow. Once you have sales, you will still be burning cash, so you have to get to positive cash flow. I think for any particular business, you have to really do a realistic budget of what you'll need to do in each of these stages and then multiply that by two or three. In our case, it was a few million dollars to get off the ground and reach profitability. I think for a technology business, ours was probably on the low side.

Money is necessary, but more isn't always better because it can be a defocus. I think that sometimes companies raise too much money. This may not be true anymore but, during the internet bubble, we saw many companies raise so much money, then end up wasting a lot of it, and doing things that weren't really getting them to their end goal faster. Fund-raising certainly is necessary, but it is not sufficient to building a successful business. It is not the end of the road, just the beginning of the road. On the other hand, I think getting a lot of customers is a really good sign that your product has a market; in addition, early sales help you leverage into new sales.

To land those first few clients, we went to the relevant trade organizations, to trade shows, and talked to customers within the industry and just made ourselves known. It was actually very easy early on because there were people who wanted the latest and greatest technologies, and so they were very interested in buying our technology because it was new and it was interesting and offered advantages over everything else that was out there. A big part of it is just making sure that people know you are out there. In our case, those initial sales were actually among the easiest. We also had credibility – our technology came from MIT and our initial team was all MIT engineers. This helped us get off the ground.

I think we were finally off the ground when we got to a point where we had predictable monthly sales. There were the initial development sales until we got the product out the door, and that was really scary because we didn't know if the product was going to work. Then we got the product out the door, and that was really exciting, but then we didn't

PRODUCT DIFFERENTIATION FROM TECHNOLOGY

know how many we were going to sell month to month. That is the next big hurdle: having a predictable stream of revenues every month so you can start to structure a profitable business. There is a period of time where you might go a month without a sale, and then you get a few more sales and you're not sure where everything is going to be month to month. It is nice to get to a steady point where you can start to really budget and forecast.

Analyzing the Market and the Risks

It is very important to understand the market need, to speak with customers, and to speak with competitors. Early on, I would just float around trade shows and talk to absolutely everyone about what we were trying to do. I think some entrepreneurs tend to be very secretive about what they are working on because they are afraid someone is going to steal their idea. What they discover is that when you actually go to sell the product down the road, it is much harder to get people to listen to you than you ever thought. You don't really have to worry about them stealing your ideas because probably they are not going to want to listen to you in the first place. There is a much bigger risk that you will develop the wrong product or go out of business. So I think it is really important to speak with potential customers – and even to speak with competitors – and to throw out the idea and get feedback. That way you can help shape how the product is developed.

It is also very important to focus on the business plan. I don't think it is important to have it formatted beautifully and to have all the details spelled out, but I think it is extremely important in terms of articulating the vision and highlighting the core financials: how are you going to make money? It is important to outline the fundamental structure of the business: who are you going to sell the product to, how much will they pay for it, and what quantity do you have to sell to reach profitability.

INSIDE THE MINDS

You have to really focus on whether the overall structure of the business makes sense. Many times people who are starting a business think mostly about the product. The very next question has to be, "If I actually want to make money, how many of that product do I need to sell in order to make it be profitable?" Very often that simple question will illuminate a fundamental problem with the business.

You have to put in a lot of thought on the assumptions in the business plan– getting things that are about right and not worrying about the tiny details, but really looking at the downside. What is the probability that things will go worse? Can you live with that? Can you afford it if that downside happens? Is the upside worth it? For example, how much money are you going to put into the business, what is the chance that you are going to lose it, and can you afford to lose that money. If so, is the upside worth losing that money? If you go down the path and things go great, but you need more money, what do you do? You have to plan for that. It will probably take a lot more money than you think. Are you going to be able to raise money at that point in time, or are you going to put yourself in a position, in subsequent investments, where you really can't afford the downside? People tend to spend a lot of time worrying about small financial risks where the big financial risk in starting a new venture is that it just goes under. I think early on it is important to always keep an eye on where the cash is in the business, and if you are going to be able to make it. This perspective requires a lot of trade-offs in the day-to-day, but it pays off, in general, comfort level and stability.

I think the big risk in starting any company is that you are not actually satisfying a need. If there is a customer willing to spend a lot of money to get the solution that you are proposing, that is a really good sign that you are satisfying a market need. If you can do that, it is a good source of funding because the terms will tend to be better than with a venture capital firm. In addition, you will know right off the bat that not only will

PRODUCT DIFFERENTIATION FROM TECHNOLOGY

you have a customer, but also that you are satisfying a real need in the marketplace.

The Entrepreneurial Management Style

Capability, credibility, and caring for people are the core elements of being a successful CEO. Capability and independence make things happen. Credibility is important in hiring people and making sales. Caring for people is what makes a good manager. The hardest part of management is dealing with the conflicts relating to people. I think the best way to cope with it is just talking it out. People are people, and so they get upset. Sometimes you have to disappoint them and that is hard to do, or you have to put someone in a different position or, even worse, you have to let them go. All of that is very difficult, but I think being open and honest is the way to get through it. It doesn't make it necessarily a whole lot easier, though.

I think my management style is entrepreneurial. I am a typical entrepreneur in that I am not afraid to be different. There is a fine line between having confidence in yourself and in the vision, as opposed to being stubborn or blind to reality. On the one hand, you want to silence the nay-sayers and tell them that this is really going to work and be successful. On the other hand, you want to be realistic, also; you don't want to believe what everyone says, but you also don't want to ignore it. If everyone tells you that there is no market for your product, you also have to listen to that. There is always that fine line, and I find myself straddling that line very often.

In terms of actually managing the business, we tend to separate strategic versus operational decisions. We try to have decisions made at the lowest possible levels where those people who have the most information are empowered to make decisions. In terms of company culture, there are no

99

frills. Everything is really straightforward, down-to-business. There's very little focus on politics; it's all about getting the job done. We have no hierarchy of perks, so all our cubicles are the same size. There are no special parking spots or anything like that. We tend to have a very casual culture. People are very comfortable speaking up and giving their opinion. We try to have a culture where people don't worry about being wrong so they are willing to take a risk. Overall, it is a very fun environment.

I think the atmosphere helps us because people feel empowered. They feel like owners in the business, so the employees take a lot of responsibility. They are not being told exactly what to do, so they are making decisions for the better good of the company. We also tend to hire people who are very smart, even if they lack experience. We take chances on people. I think that has also helped us out a great deal. There has been a lot of opportunity for growth for all of the employees as they come in.

We also try to be very careful about how we place people. I think one of the most important decisions that the senior managers make is not just who to hire but what projects to put people on. We do that by an assessment of their capabilities. One thing that becomes really obvious when you start a business is how incredibly varied people's capabilities are. You can find somebody who is absolutely brilliant in one area and completely incompetent in another area. You have to make sure that they are in the position where they are brilliant because that is good for the company, it is good for them, and everything is smooth sailing. Finding the right position for each person is extremely important, and it becomes pretty obvious.

Customer service, for example, is extremely important. My sense is that it is very hard to teach someone truly good customer service. They either have it in them or they don't. You can see this sense of concern for the

PRODUCT DIFFERENTIATION FROM TECHNOLOGY

customer in any position within the organization, from the receptionist who offers to take someone's coat to the Vice President who stays late to make sure the shipment is correct.

I think you can generally tell when you interview whether or not someone has an entrepreneurial spirit. Our country's culture over the last few years has tended to revere the entrepreneurial spirit, so I think people generally tend to be more entrepreneurial today than they were 20 years ago. They are more excited about taking a risk and making that work, whereas I think it was much harder 20 years ago to get someone to buy into a small start-up. Today there is a much bigger pool of potential employees interested in "taking the plunge." I think enough people have been successful now that others want to do it. It's not for everyone, though. People have to be comfortable taking a risk, and that is not for everyone. They also have to be comfortable living in an environment where they have to do a lot of things themselves because there is nobody else to do it for them. Sometimes we make mistakes and hire people who don't really have that spirit, and they don't last long.

I think an overall entrepreneurial environment makes everyone feel like owners. It makes them feel more loyal to the organization and its mission. They grow with the organization, they are a part of making things happen, and their decisions make a difference to the success of the business. Their satisfaction comes from the impact they have on building a thriving business.

Goals and Strategy

We had two missions when we founded our company. One was to make money, and the other was to have fun doing it. For other companies, like non-profit organizations, they often have the more worthy goal of helping people. We didn't have that goal explicitly, but we do take great

INSIDE THE MINDS

satisfaction in just the simple fact of providing jobs and helping the economy.

On a personal level, I think there is a tremendous amount of fulfillment that comes from creating something where before there was nothing. I think, generally, entrepreneurs get a big kick out of just making things happen, because early on in a business something can go from being a thought in your mind to actual execution very quickly. It's very exciting to have things happen so quickly.

In fact, the entrepreneur can fall into a trap of getting "hooked" on activity. The tendency is always to focus on execution, so occasionally you have to set aside time for strategic thinking. We have regular board meetings, which give us feedback from people who are not involved in the day-to-day issues and can provide some perspective. Just preparing for the board meetings is very valuable in that it gets the management team thinking about the bigger picture. Even if we never actually had the board meeting, we would get a lot out of the preparation, including the discussions that take place as part of the preparation. On top of all that, the meetings are incredibly useful because the board has its own unique perspective. They can really help clarify our thinking. We have walked out of board meetings with a completely different opinion than when we walked in.

In terms of setting broad strategies for the business, I think a key strategy for running a new small business is not trying to do what large companies can do better, but trying to stick to the things that smaller businesses can do better. Small companies have two advantages. One is development; small companies can do much better core, basic, early-stage fundamental development. Smaller businesses are also much better at creating new markets. Large companies tend to be much better at making incremental improvements to existing products. They listen to what customers have to say and they make incremental improvements to

102

PRODUCT DIFFERENTIATION FROM TECHNOLOGY

those products, but they tend to not be very good at creating entirely new markets that didn't exist before.

Overall, small companies tend to be much more comfortable embracing change. Change has been part of our company culture since the beginning. We were really driving the change from the beginning, and even now we are still at a size where that is very much a part of our inbred culture. We try to be at the leading edge so that we are defining how the industry is changing. We want to be in control of it, not watching everybody else change around us – we want to be the ones making it change.

We have seen a lot of competitors come and go, generally due to poor strategy, inferior technology, and sloppy execution. From the surviving companies we have seen pricing pressures, which I think is very natural. In many industries, the products tend to become faster, better, cheaper and that is what we see in our own industry. From a strategic point of view, we believe we are in a very advantageous position because we believe that our technology has fundamental characteristics that will give us an advantage in pushing the products to be ever faster, better and cheaper. It's important in selecting the technology at the outset to imagine what forces will come to play in the industry, and make a fair assessment as to whether that technology will be a surviving technology. It's not as important that you have the best product initially as it is that you have the best technology to drive and lead the industry.

Keys to Success

The key to success is initially to pick the right business. What I mean by that is a business where you are going to be able to make money. You need to be able to write a short Income Statement on the back of an envelope that shows how you can be profitable. The second is making

INSIDE THE MINDS

sure that the product solves a real problem – that it is not a solution looking for a problem, but that it actually solves a problem that somebody is going to be willing to pay for. Market assessment is a critical component of this – making sure that there is a market need and looking at the market size to make sure that somebody in the world who cares about it has the resources to pay for it. Third is picking good people and putting them in the right positions. This is not easy, so you have to allow for mistakes and be willing to make changes.

Sales are absolutely critical because for a company in the initial phase of start-up, it is very important what customers have to say. You need to hear their objections and hear why they do or don't want to buy the product. It's as important to talk to those who don't want to buy as to those who do want to buy. Selling is key for the CEO early on because it helps define product; it helps define the marketing strategy, product positioning, and also the development strategy.

Finally, you have to believe in your product. I strongly believe in what we are offering, so I think that really helps. I have a passion for it and try to show that passion. I also try to build credibility with the people I encounter, so that they believe me. I think that if I am honest and open by freely sharing information in order to build credibility, then my belief in this vision has credibility.

Stumbling Blocks

There are two fundamental fatal errors that an entrepreneur can make. Misinterpreting the market need is one – believing that there is a market need where there really isn't. Market assessment is very important. The best exercise for an entrepreneur is to try to pre-sell the product to potential customers, outlining a set of specifications and a timeline when

PRODUCT DIFFERENTIATION FROM TECHNOLOGY

the product will be ready. This can highlight a lot of the potential difficulties in ultimately selling the product.

Another enormous risk is running out of money or spending all your time as CEO raising money. I think a lot of companies get into that mode, so you spend all your time raising money and no time running the business. There needs to be a focus on running the business, developing and selling product, and reaching profitability. Raising money is a necessary evil, but it costs the CEO's time, which is one of the company's most valuable resources. So the less money the company needs to raise, the more time the CEO will have to run the business. Our overall philosophy has been to focus on running a business and having the excitement in the business revolve around being successful and having the product be successful and generating sales – not around having fancy offices and things like that. We have been able to attract very good people by having the appeal be in the product and the technology and the success of the product, not around the other more superficial aspects. By doing that, we have been able to conserve our resources so that we don't have to spend all our time raising money. As I said before, this culture is not for everyone, but it has thankfully not been a barrier to us hiring great employees.

I think there are two key smaller stumbling blocks that entrepreneurs face. One is general, while the other is more specific. I think a general pitfall is a lack of focus. I think it is very easy early on to go down a million different paths because there is so much potential with the technology, and there are all these exciting things you can do with it. This is a real risk, particularly because usually the initial employees are all technical and often are creative; so they get more excited about pursuing new activities than about making incremental developments on something old. You have to get out of the mode of "well, let's just do it because we can" and look at your real goal: "We want to get to profitability and we want to get there fast so, yes, it would be really cool

105

to do that project, but we are not going to do it." You have to become very good at managing your time, not just as an individual but as a company, to keep the rest of the world from trying to defocus you and get you off your path. The ultimate goal, which is to create a product and make money, has to be at the forefront of everyone's mind on a day-to-day basis.

The second stumbling block is pricing. Generally, I think new companies tend to under price their products. You tend to undersell the value proposition because you are just so grateful to have an interested customer. At the end of the day, when you add in all the costs of making your product, selling your product, and servicing your product, it will be twice as high as you initially thought. That was a mistake that we came very close to making. We happened to be saved at the last minute, and we were very lucky.

Concerns and Advice

As an entrepreneur, I have several worries. Initially it was that it wouldn't work – that there would be problems with the technology once it actually got into the marketplace, or that the market we were creating would never materialize. I think that whenever you are creating a new market this worry exists; you never know if there's a real market until you get the product out there. The other risk, which still lingers today, is that a new technology that we don't know about may come out that is much better. That is always really scary. And the only way I know of to reduce this risk is to try to be aware of any new technologies as they come out.

In terms of looking back, I think there are two things I would have done differently. One is to scale-up our sales and marketing efforts sooner. We could have been more aggressive on selling and marketing the product

PRODUCT DIFFERENTIATION FROM TECHNOLOGY

once we first got it out the door. We tended to do things serially, so we first developed a product and then started to do a low-level sales process, and I think we could have really gotten the sales process going much sooner. In our defense, we wanted to be absolutely sure that the product quality was adequate, and we didn't want to spend all our time fighting fires, but we could have learned a lot by selling the product faster. And we would have reached our subsequent milestones faster. There's ultimately no way to perfect the product in-house. At a certain point it just has to be put in the hands of the customer, so you can get meaningful feedback that will drive help shape product development and marketing efforts going forward. Of course, there has to be a balance. The downside of releasing a product before it is ready is huge. But, in our case, we made the mistake of ramping up sales too slowly in the first year or two.

The other thing I would do differently relates to my personal management style. I think I would delegate sooner. Delegating is something that is hard for many entrepreneurs because you are used to doing everything yourself, and you are used to being the center of everything. It's hard to let go because you think nobody is going to do it as well as you. This is erroneous thinking, because (1) often the other person will do a better job, or can take your good thoughts and add their own ideas; and (2) even if they don't do a better job, there are often more important things for you to do with your time. Now, in retrospect, I think I could have leveraged my own capabilities much better by delegating sooner. Of course, it's critical to have good employees who you trust, otherwise you'll never be comfortable delegating. If you're not comfortable delegating, then you have to do some soul-searching to see if it's because you don't want to give up control or because you need to shuffle some of the employees. Ultimately, though, it's the only way to build the business. Whenever I feel uncomfortable giving a task to someone else, I try to imagine whether the CEO of a billion-dollar business would be doing that task themselves. I figure that if they can be comfortable delegating such a task then I should be too.

107

The best piece of overall advice I've received – and it also applies to business – is to seize the opportunity. You may think that some opportunity that you are faced with may come back, but in fact it may not. In terms of business, you obviously need to be well educated in order to take advantage of an appropriate opportunity and be smart about it, not just crazy. But if you know a lot about the market, or make the effort to do so, you can position yourself to be prepared to be opportunistic. Then when that opportunity comes up, you can act quickly and gain advantage. We tend to be very opportunistic, and when things come along, even if they weren't in the schedule, if we feel well educated about it, we tend to seize that opportunity. This only works as part of some larger strategic plan. But if you have a strong strategic vision and stay well educated, you can find great opportunities just by keeping your eyes open and remaining open to the idea of change. That's really how we started our business in the first place. I wanted to find a technology that could be used to create a large market, and I searched for an entire year, kissing a lot of frogs before I found it. But once I found it and realized that we could have a product with excellent differentiation based on the core technology, I got our team together and we founded the business within a few weeks. Once the strategic pieces are in place, it's just a matter of execution.

Marina Hatsopoulos, CEO and Co-founder of Z Corporation, has an M.S. from MIT in Mechanical Engineering. She spent several years on Wall Street and then worked for several high-tech companies in mergers and acquisitions, marketing and management prior to starting up Z Corporation.

Marina graduated with a B.A. in Pure Mathematics and a B.A. in Music from Brown University in 1987 (Phi Beta Kappa, Magna Cum Laude, Mathematics Prize, and Faculty Fellowship). She then worked in corporate finance for the oil and gas industry at The Chase Manhattan

PRODUCT DIFFERENTIATION FROM TECHNOLOGY

Bank in New York, negotiating $2.5 billion in financing deals. In 1990 she pursued more operational roles in her work at various Thermo Electron Corporation subsidiaries, heading up special projects in mergers and acquisitions, marketing and project management. She received her M.S. in Mechanical Engineering from MIT in 1993 (Sigma Xi). During this time she also completed four major rehabilitations with a market value of $4.5 million, including architectural layout, interior and exterior design, and construction management. She continued to consult at Thermo Electron while actively searching for a business to manage.

In 1994, she visited the MIT Technology Licensing Office with the objective of finding a new technology to commercialize. Upon being introduced to MIT's 3D Printing technology, she negotiated the license to the patents from MIT and founded Z Corporation along with Walter Bornhorst (PhD, MIT '66), and the inventors of the new technology, Jim Bredt (PhD, MIT '94) and Tim Anderson.

She is currently CEO and a Director of Z Corporation. She is also a member of the Committee on Finance and Investment and a member of the Audit Committee of the American Society of Mechanical Engineers (ASME). She was honored with Mass. High Tech's All-Star Award for Hardware in 2001. She was selected in 2002 to be a charter member of the Creative Economy Council, a select group of New England leaders representing business, government and the arts community led by the President of the Federal Reserve Bank of Boston, whose purpose is to increase investment in New England's creative economy to stimulate economic growth.

Making It Up As You Go

Kevin D. Grauman
The Outsource Group, LLC
President & CEO

Beginning at the Beginning

Passion!

There are many reasons why entrepreneurs start their businesses, but they are all for naught without PASSION! Clearly, there must be an inherent perception of a compelling market opportunity or in a belief that you can do "it" better than most, but without the passion to want to cause it to happen, the chances of success will be virtually zero.

Understanding what it is and how to reign it in have, for the longest time, stumped many analysts, from the pure academicians to the brightest business consultants. Some have attempted to dissect it into component elements and then to further dismember those sub-elements. The truth of it, though, is that you (somehow) know when it is there – it's the stuff that keeps you up at night; it's the innate ability to "sell" the concept or idea and to do so to anyone who will lend an ear; it's the perception of uncompromised competence; and it's a belief that failure is not a contemplated option.

Once you recognize that you have this passion, it is necessary to foster it, to nurture it, and to feed its appetite – by beginning the metamorphosis from idea to reality; in other words, growing your company.

Stay Real and Avoid Surprises
The most important thing about the process, though, is to be realistic. Often there's a tendency to make *pie-in-the-sky* extrapolations of the expected realities, and it's fatally damaging if you don't focus on the "real" reality of things. Don't let yourself be romanced by what could be and what should be instead of what is. Honest realism, I think, is, therefore essential.

Additionally, it *is* important to sweat the details. Surprises, apart from being very unpleasant and rather time-consuming, result in a loss of focus, they erode confidence (passion, too), and they occur, most often, as a product of bad planning. The decision to start a business is a tactical one, and you have to be tactically focused, in excruciating detail. Nothing should be considered to be too small. And, the more you focus in on those small details, the more successful you'll likely be and surprises will be less apt to occur – at least certainly not to the degree and severity that they do for the unprepared.

I think, too, that if you do your research correctly and with focus, unwanted, influential surprises will be limited. Now, it would be naïve to suggest that you can plan or prepare yourself from being surprised at all, but this planning and preparation, if done correctly and intelligently, will mitigate much. Therefore, in your financial budgeting and modeling, try to work on both a worst-case scenario and a best-case scenario. The ultimate reality will probably be somewhere in between, but if you deal honestly with both extreme outcomes, both sides of the coin, then the likelihood of your being surprised will be low. (As a side-bar, once you have modeled your worst-case scenario, make sure that you have secured adequate financial resources if this eventuality was to occur – otherwise there is a very high probability that it will significantly hinder – or deplete altogether – your ability to launch your business.)

"The Plan"
One proven method for planning is to align yourself with some trusted advisors who are top-shelf, ethical, successful players in their own industries– and to try to learn from and mimic those "best" business practices. I think ethics is what it's all about at the end of the day, so researching and aligning yourself with competent, relevant, and trusted advisors, who possess integrity, cannot be overstressed. This includes financial people, banking people, marketing people, people with expertise in whatever product, or service, that you are attempting to bring to market – the whole gamut. Try to be smart about their selection and use a rifle, not a shotgun, approach in their selection. Remember, too,

that it's all about quality, not quantity, and the ultimate goal is to leverage what has worked for them, not to attempt to reinvent the wheel for yourself and your business.

I'm still not convinced that merely writing a traditional business plan is necessarily a have-to-have in the big scheme of things. In concept only, it certainly is nice to have and, for those who require the structure and discipline to succinctly define and refine the concept and the model, it may prove to be critically important. Regardless of the formality of it, though, be honest with yourself by trying not to disguise reality. One has to be clear in one's own mind as to what the overall market opportunities are, what the competitive landscape looks like, and, understanding both, how to succeed. The business plan is an important tool in this regard if it's utilized correctly, but often it's not. It needs to become and remain a living document, constantly being updated by the changing landscape and continuing to provide both a strategic and tactical roadmap that bridges the past with the future. Instead of regarding it as another chore to perform, drop the "business" part of it, and merely think of it as "the plan". And, we all know how important it is to have "a plan"!

Additionally, it's very necessary to regularly communicate this plan (a.k.a. the company's strategic vision) – I'd say at least once every quarter, to individuals in the company, on a very formal basis. Communicating is not an option, but should be viewed as necessary to align all company members with "the plan". It needs to be regular, concise, and comprehensive.

Whatever it Takes
In the early days, the indelible start-up phase, CEO is merely a title. You have to do pretty much everything in order to keep your cost side of the equation in check. Mostly, because there is no one else available to do it, and, more importantly, because you care. But, as you become more successful and the business starts to take shape, the only way you can

grow the company tangibly and strategically is to allow other people to step into those operations and tactical roles Once you do that, you're then in a position to focus strategically, for, I'd say, a goal of 85 to 90 percent of your time, and everyone benefits, even you.

Letting go is a very, very hard decision, because, obviously, "no one can do it as well" as you can, at least perceptively. I "let go" about two-and-a-half years ago, and it was probably one of the best decisions of my life. But it was probably one of the hardest decisions to have made, because you're trusting that someone else will have the same passion, competence, and responsibility as you have, and that's a gamble. Sometimes it works and sometimes it doesn't, and if it doesn't, you end up going back into that role. But, without moving out of that role (albeit temporarily for some), you have no way of becoming more strategic in the way that you need to grow your business; there's absolutely no way. So you have to make a tangible decision, a focused, excruciatingly painful decision – but it's all for good; it's not a bad thing.

Key Resources

There really are only four key resources upon which executive managers can and should focus their internal efforts: time, money, technology, and people. They are all mutually exclusive, on one level, but are substantially interconnected on another. And no single resource should be viewed as more important, or as requiring more attention, than any other.

People
Clearly, people are critical to the success of any enterprise. They are your eyes and ears in the marketplace, they listen to your clients/customers, they act as your proxy when you are not present, they are sensitive to your "underbelly", and they are your best marketers. And, if you are

attempting to make critical decisions regarding the hiring of people, make sure that you spend an enormous amount of time focused, initially, in the recruitment effort. It would be valuable to "profile" the personality characteristics that you feel will be most valuable to the future of your business, and to target your hiring with that in mind. Make sure that the ethics and integrity that you regularly expound are embraced by those who you are hiring as your disciples. And always be honest with your current and prospective employees; don't lie. Be respectful, reward maturity, do not tolerate "drama", nurture competence, encourage the making of mistakes (we all hate to fail, anyway!), and foster an environment where honest and regular communication is the norm.

Money

It seems trite to mention it, but money (for most) is the "end game"; ultimately it is the reason for assuming all of the business risks, for the sleepless nights, and for embracing the associated "opportunity cost". It, too, is the measure by which the relative success of the enterprise is determined over time. Consequently, intimately understanding the fiscal side of the house is critical to success of the business enterprise, since these tactical and strategic successes are mostly referenced in monetary terms, whether they be $'s or %'s – revenue, gross margin, net cash-flow, margin contribution, EBITDA, and net profit, to name just a few. Ensuring that you fully understand the metrics of what it's going to take to get your business to your various pre-determined milestones is an important prerequisite to actually achieving these milestones. If you do not have a formal training in this regard, make sure that one of your trusted advisors and one of your initial key-hires have both the aptitudes and the abilities to keep you fully apprised of the fiscal "goings-on". If you do not, it is probable that you will not fully have your finger on the pulse of your business, and you will likely be less than adequately equipped to proactively manage it.

Clearly, a key element of this proactive management effort is to ensure that you have adequate funding (or the pre-negotiated facilities for it) in place to reach each milestone, with reference to both the best-case and worst-case business-climate scenarios that were previously mentioned. On the low side, worst-case scenario, if nothing happens, or if very little happens, how do you cope with that? And on the high side, what happens if growth is explosive? How do you deal with that? Both can be problems for you and both require capital resources, without which the outcomes will be similar.

Time
Time is the least controllable of the key resources that you will be required to manage. But, without your dedicated attention to it, there is a tendency to be bogged down by the details, causing you to favor one direction versus another based on your crisis-of-the-moment. The ultimate goal is to prioritize your time: both regarding the extent to which it is available to your business, and as it pertains to the weighting associated with the items that present themselves (i.e., the relative importance of each).

Having a good balance between your working life and your "other" life is very necessary to enable you to avoid becoming so immersed in, and consumed by, your business that your effectiveness in it is not readily evident, or no longer becomes the priority. I very often encounter entrepreneurs who work seven days a week for fifteen hour days trying to get everything done. I very seldom witness success, though. The goal, clearly, is to work on the business (strategic), not in the business (tactical), and to work smarter (strategic), not harder (tactical).

Technology
It would be naïve on my part to propose that technology, as a resource, is a key component in *every* new business. However, my hope is that, to the extent that current and relevant technology can be embraced, it should

be. And, not merely for the sake of the technology, but to enhance productivity, to effectively and efficiently manage and provide ready access to data, to enable quick response times, to communicate well and quickly, to become educated and to educate, and, in general, to get the message out.

The overriding concept that I am proposing is that, in order to operate at the highest levels of efficiency, and to promote maximum effectiveness, relevant and current technology should be embraced, implemented, and utilized on a wholesale level and by all employees in the company. In today's world the costs of not doing so are too great

The People Equation

Managing With Your Gut
Finding and hiring the right people is all about your gut, at least initially. I think there are some metrics that can be employed (psychological testing or personality profiling, if you wish), but, for the most part, it's a gut feel based on what you perceive to be valuable to you, from a personality standpoint and from a competence standpoint. You can generally get a sense of what someone is going to be like straight out of the box if you do your homework and extrapolate it into the interviewing process. And it is likely to be a very arduous process if you don't do it right!

My management style is involved and complex, but it has noticeably metamorphosized over time, never really being static. I much prefer a very flat organizational structure and a very open communication style within our company. I have lived the alternative, very unhappily. Our environment nurtures competence and participation, not title. Any good idea is, at least, evaluated, based on its merits, not dismissed. Don't confuse this with management by consensus. It is not. Instead, it involves

118

participation by all relevant parties. Ultimately, somebody has to be in charge, but the information flow needs to be, and is, nurtured. People are valued based on their input and participation in real, tangible, practical, and measurable terms that result in an impact in our organization. If participants feel they're making a difference, they'll actively, continuously and honestly participate and be passionate about doing so; if they feel that others have the goal of beating them up all the time, they're not going to participate very well. In a nutshell (at least for me), it's all about valuing individual employees, listening to what they have to say, and changing course if the ideas have merit. I call it "change management".

Clearly, the entrepreneurial mindset is recognized as being more risk-prone, and it is one that is comfortable with this much higher level of risk. With this comes more multi-tasking, and since participants in this environment usually wear many more functional hats than they would otherwise, the apparent lack of structure is oftentimes misinterpreted by those outside of it. It is usually associated with chaos, but nothing could be further from reality. The individual decisions that are made by these multi-taskers tend to have a greater impact on the business as a whole because fewer individuals make them and do so more often. Consequently, the resultant highs are higher and the lows are lower in this entrepreneurial environment – it's more of a peak and valley scenario. And, this setting is not for everybody, but for those who participate in it, I'd say the juices flow a lot more often and with greater intensity. It's excitement, demoralization, and hoopla much of the time, with no real predictability associated with the "flavor of the moment" and freneticism being the common activity.

Moths to a Flame
As a leader, you have to actually feel and live the ideal. People will be attracted to the passion, I think, to the energy and to the excitement. And, if you're honest about it, in wholesale fashion, without regard for the

audience, it feeds on itself, and the whole becomes greater than sum of each individual. Of paramount importance, though, one must provide an ethical character to the company, so that you and all those that are associated with it are beyond reproach with nothing to hide, least of all the truth. This requires a full sharing of information. If there's good news, great; if there's bad news, everybody needs to know about it. There's no point in holding onto it for the purposes of ownership or protection. The overall mantra should be to manage everybody's expectations, without surprises.

I think that a common element of the average workplace is dysfunction, which is mostly a product of the drama that people feel that they need to create around themselves – the politics that people perpetrate. It feeds on itself, and it's pretty destructive. So if you can get rid of the negative intangibles (the politics and the drama), and focus more on constructively managing everybody's expectations, I think everybody will be better off for that, especially the company. Remarkably, the mere act of not willing to tolerate it, speaks volumes for the passionate dedication to success. And, simply put, people will be unwilling to follow if they feel that they are being deceived, minimized, or traumatized.

Competence is Vital; But What is It?
Competence is probably one of the hardest concepts or personality traits to identify, or to hire, but it is absolutely vital to the success of your business. Without it, all that you have hired are a bunch of resumes and you are likely to become really experienced at doing so.

What is it, though, and what it is not? Most definitely it is street smarts – the ability to think on your feet, to make rational decisions with less than perfect information. It is a willingness to make mistakes; it is the exuding of an air of confidence, without being overbearing; it is an acknowledgement that there is more to learn than is known; it is the ability to apologize without a needed excuse; it is the embracing of the continual need for constructive communication; and it is attempting to always be relevant.

Measuring Success – How Do You Know You've Arrived

I measure success on the faces of the people with whom I work, and the energy that they expend in the process. I look at the results of what they do, how they do it, how they feel about what they're doing, how others feel about working with them, whether they are genuine, and the extent of both their passion and of their need to make excuses. If all of those are very positive, then I consider a success to have been achieved.

As executive managers, we have an enormous responsibility to those who work "for" us and to those that are dependent upon those who work "for" us. We are responsible, to a large degree, for the quality of those lives, and for the extent to which financial resources are available to those people. Consequently, I measure success in two ways: obviously, there is a need to meet or exceed the business's financial goals – I see this as more of a one dimensional goal, since you either get there or you don't, and the yardstick is financial. The second measure is both deeper and broader in scope and in implication. It is a cumulative measure of the positive impacts that building the business has had on the lives of those who have invested their efforts – the number of first-time homeowners that have been created while working at the company, the number of children of employees who have excelled academically or athletically, where and for how long vacations are taken, etc.

Now, it's obviously important to have a profitable company – don't get me wrong – but it's not the primary motivator, and it certainly isn't mine. Clearly, most people, including business gurus, the media and academia, measure business success in monetary terms. However, operating and living in an environment where excessive consumption is revered, as is certainly the American way, it is not difficult to become a "hamster on a treadmill" – working to live to work to live. The begging question becomes: "How much is enough for me?" And, achieving "enough" should be viewed as having accomplished success, at least in pure monetary terms.

Recent and Future Changes

Explosion of the Internet
Over the past five years or so, companies-at-large have experienced one of the most dramatic revolutions in the history of business and enterprise: the introduction and continued improvement of e-Business to enable revenue growth, education, information flows, productivity enhancements, and increased competitive advantages.

This revolution has resulted in a wholesale move by businesses to embrace technology on the web. In my view, any business owner or executive manager who is not thinking about implementing web-based technology to enhance their operations is out of business, at least in the medium-term.

It's All About Service
I think that most companies today, certainly as it applies in the United States, are in the service business, whether they acknowledge it or not. And, while they embrace the "move to the web" as their competitive advantage, eventually everyone will have done so. Consequently, a dedicated focus towards, and a training of, superior customer service is critical for long-term survival and ultimate success. The paradigm shift will be one from reactive to proactive behavior, with business consumers ultimately being the primary focus (as it should always have been, in the first place).

In order for this to occur, I think, too, as it applies to the hiring of employees-at-large, you're likely to see less focus on résumé competence and more focus on psychological profiling – a search for knowledge workers as opposed to résumé workers. The traditional organizational chart will, therefore, be replaced by a more dynamic three-dimensional model, where the customer is at the core, and progressive layers of competence will be available to that customer as it relates to service. The customer is free to "peel the layers" outwardly, in an effort to tap the complexity of the feedback that is being requested.

Where's The Golden Goose?

As far as the business horizon is concerned, predicting the next "golden goose" is proving to be next to impossible. Also, the recent bursting of the Internet bubble has jaded many business futurists, certainly as it pertains to new and exciting concepts, and to the point where there is much more predictability for things to come. I, too, do not believe that we will see any significant change in the way that business is being done today, other than a more wholesale use of the Internet and a more dedicated focus towards proactive customer service. Maybe (at least there is always the wish) executive managers will, instead, begin to re-define for themselves the true meaning of success!

Kevin D. Grauman is a respected and skilled specialist in the field of finance and outsourced human resources administration. His practical and theoretical expertise extends to financial resource management, payroll accounting, employee benefits administration and human resources management, transliterate on local, regional, national and international levels. He champions efficiency and compliance, primarily in favor of "non-large" employers, and regularly consults with these employers regarding wages and hours, fair employment practice, compensation, labor relations, employee benefits, and personnel management.

Establishing the Need

David R. Cassell
Consultants' Choice, Inc.
Chairman & CEO

So You Think You Want To Start Your Own Business!

I encourage you to do so. I have started two businesses in the last twenty years, and they have been the most rewarding experiences of my life. It is important that you know what you are getting into, and I will relate some of my personal experiences that will hopefully help in your endeavor. I will address this subject by discussing the following topics:

Establishing a Need and a Vision
Developing a Plan
Obtaining Funding
Hiring the Right People with the Right Incentives
Executing the Plan
Your Personal Life
Conclusion

Establishing a Need and Vision

First, to be successful in business, you have to fill a need. You have to offer something different, better, or less expensive. You have to have reasons why what you are doing is better than what other people in the market are providing, and you must have a vision as to how your product or service is going to be successful.

In order to have a believable, sellable vision, you also need knowledge of the industry that you are about to enter. I have seen many people make the mistake of undertaking a new business with no experience in that particular industry. Sometimes things appear to be easy and starting a new business is a difficult way to learn how important knowledge and experience are to achieving your ultimate success.

ESTABLISHING THE NEED

When I started my first business in 1982, the need was easy to determine. There was a tremendous shortage of good technical people in Information Technology (called Data Processing back then). The Information Technology Services industry was in its infancy. I was aware of this problem because I had spent the last fifteen years selling computer systems for IBM. I was paid when the systems were installed, not when they were sold. In many cases, the delivery of the equipment was delayed because the clients did not have enough resource available to get the work done that justified bringing in the new systems. I would get involved in helping them find the resources on a contract basis.

My vision was to create a company that would recruit good technical resources who had no interest or skills in management and provide them with the ability to make more money by providing their technical services to the clients on an as needed basis. We would then be able to offer technical services to the prospective clients that would allow them to realize savings to their organizations sooner by utilizing our services. We spent the majority of our selling time convincing the clients that this new approach was a significant benefit to them.

My second business was started in late 1997. The situation was similar to 1982, in that there was even a greater shortage of Information Technology skills. The big difference was that we were now in a mature industry with too many companies competing for the same business. Using Information Technology service providers was an accepted practice by most organizations. Their challenge was finding Information Technology Service Providers that could actually produce qualified resources at a reasonable price. Our vision was to recruit the best technical resources by providing a new employer/employee paradigm. This paradigm recognized that the consultants were going to be our major asset and setting up a model that recognized this fact. We had an open paradigm that treated all of our employees the same. They were paid a flat percentage of the bill rate to the client and had the opportunity to earn equity in our company. The consultants were involved in the decision making process in our company and were viewed by the internal sales and recruiting people in our organization as the major asset in our company. In order to be able to deliver these resources to the marketplace at reasonable rates, we had to control our internal costs. We operate in Class B office space and have a very flat organization. Needless to say, we became the employer of choice in the markets in which we were doing business. Finding clients was easy as we were able to produce the best resource at reasonable rates.

Most entrepreneurs are visionaries. I think that's probably the one thing that stands out. No matter what I'm doing, or what I'm looking at, I'm always wondering, "Is there a better way to do this?" Your vision needs to be clear, concise, and understandable to someone outside of your industry. You must be able to articulate the vision with a passion as to why your vision will be successful and a commitment to do whatever is necessary to accomplish your goals. As Vince Lombardi said, "A man can be a great as he wants to be. If you believe in yourself and have the courage, the determination, the dedication, the competitive drive and if your are willing to sacrifice the little things in life and pay the price for the things that are worthwhile, it can be done". To have this courage, determination, dedication and competitive drive, you must have a vision that you are passionate about. This will be very important in obtaining funding, hiring the right people, closing business and successfully executing your plan.

Developing a Plan

You have to do a business plan and a cash flow plan. The cash flow plan is very important; as this will help you to determine how much money you will need to successfully start your business. You need to put together a five-year plan, especially if you're going out to raise money.

ESTABLISHING THE NEED

In this marketplace, you're lucky if you can figure out what's going to happen twelve months from today, let alone five years out. But to raise capital to start your business, potential investors are going to be interested in the long-term prospects of your venture, as this will help them determine a potential return on their investment.

You are fortunate today to have wonderful tools like Lotus and Excel available to develop your financial plan. The great thing about these tools is that it is very easy to tweak the model as you see holes in your plan. I can assure you that there will be many iterations of your Financial Plan before you reach a plan that you feel comfortable with and, more importantly, a plan that your potential investors will feel comfortable with.

In 1981 during our vision and planning phases, our spreadsheets were all done manually. There were two years of monthly data and three more years of quarterly data. Every time we made a change, we had to redo all the rows and columns by hand. We had a roomful of paper by the time we were finished.

An important thing to remember is that all of us entrepreneurs have a tendency to be incredibly optimistic about how well things are going to go and how quickly success is going to come. I have found that the best thing to do is to take whatever you think you are going to do revenue-wise and cut it in half, and take whatever you have for expenses and double that figure to do your cash planning up front. This is particularly applicable for the first year of your plan. One of the things that hurts many new businesses is that they do not raise enough money up front to adequately provide for the needs of the business in the first few months and years of the business. Once you've run into trouble and run out of money, it is difficult to go out and raise additional money. So in the planning phase, you have to be careful and conservative in your estimates of how quickly things are going to happen. You must provide

129

for significantly more expenses than what you originally anticipated. If you do that, you should be in good shape.

In my mind, the primary purpose of a long-term plan is to raise money to start your venture. The short-term plan (first twelve months) is an important road map that you should always keep current to twelve months. It is guaranteed that you will face significant changes in your plan as the world economy evolves and the economic environment improves.

Obtaining Funding

If you are fortunate enough to be independently wealthy, you can skip this topic. For the majority of us, starting a new business means taking risk, making sacrifices, and obtaining enough funds to insure that you survive the start-up of the business venture. Most entrepreneurs make the mistake of thinking that banks will loan them the money to start their businesses. This is not true unless you have enough assets to secure the money that you want to borrow. If you have the assets to secure the loan, then you probably do not need the loan. My experience has been that banks will lend you money when you are consistently profitable with a positive cash flow. This again begs the question, if you are consistently profitable with a positive cash flow, why do you need to borrow money? In other words, forget the banks until your business has matured.

The best places to go for funding are friends and business associates. You are dealing with people who know you and believe that you are credible because of experiences they have had with you. You will get the best terms and your life will be easier in the first few months. It is important that some of these investors have business experience as they can provide sage advice as you undertake your venture. As smart as you

ESTABLISHING THE NEED

think you are, I can assure you that there will be times that you will want sound advise and counsel.

One of the most important things that potential investors are going to be looking for is the amount of risk and sacrifice that you personally are willing to take. If the risk is low or non-existent in the eyes of your potential investors, the odds are that they will not provide you with the money that you need. Why should they take a risk on investing in you when you do not have enough confidence in yourself to put yourself at risk?

If your friends and business associates cannot provide the necessary funding, you will be forced into the venture capital marketplace. This is not a good place to be in today's economic environment as many of these firms have suffered considerable losses because of bad investments made toward the end of the last century, particularly in the telecommunication, high tech, and information technology service arenas.

There are others more qualified to discuss the alternate forms of funding in more detail, as I have had the fortune of using friends and business associates in my two ventures. In my first venture, I was fortunate to raise money from client officers and their friends and associates from my contacts developed through my job at IBM. In the second start up, I was able to raise the necessary funds from my employees as a result of allowing them to earn equity in the company by helping to fund the start up costs.

Hiring the Right People with the Right Incentives

One key thing that leads to success in a new business, particularly in the early stages, is hiring people you have confidence in to get the job done. You have to let them know what the job is, and then pretty much leave

131

them alone. Micromanagement, when starting a business, does not work in my experience. You have try to hire people you have confidence in and people better than yourself. Then you have to let them do their thing. You have to continuously motivate them, provide them with the necessary tools, and give them advice and counsel on an as needed basis. Obviously you have to watch what they're doing, and if they're doing something to jeopardize the success of the business, then you have to step in.

One of the most important characteristics to look for in candidates is a positive attitude and positive outlook on life. This is particularly important now because of all the negative news in the media. There are two ways of looking at everything: What can go right? and What can go wrong? I think you need to hire people that focus on what can go right. Obviously you have to be able to deal with the things that go wrong, but the major emphasis has to be on the positive. Charles Twindoll's quote is appropriate to this topic:

"Attitude. The longer I live the more I realize the impact of Attitude on life. Attitude to me is more important than the past, than education, than money, than circumstances, than failures, than success, than what other people think or say or do. It is more important than appearance, giftedness or skill. It will make or break a company, a church, a home. The remarkable thing is we have a choice every day regarding the Attitude we will embrace for that day. We cannot change our past...we cannot change the fact that people will act in a certain way. We cannot change the inevitable. The only thing we can do is plan on the one string we have and that is our Attitude. I am convinced that life is 10 percent what happens to me and 90 percent how I react to it. And so it is with you...we are in charge of our Attitudes."

In order to find the right people to join your team, you have to have a clear vision of where you are going. You have to have a vision and you

ESTABLISHING THE NEED

have to be passionate about that vision. You have to be able to sell that vision to other people. You have to determine during the interview process if your candidates understand and accept your vision and can get passionate about the mission. I also believe that in order to get the kind of people that you really need to be successful in business, you have to look at the needs of each individual that you hire. You have to develop a win-win relationship with every individual. The best advice I can give you is that to be successful and happy, you have to take care of your people. You have to make them believe that you truly care about them.

Do not hesitate to give your key people the opportunity to earn equity in your business. This was an absolutely critical part of our success in making the Inc. 500 list as the 23rd fastest growing company in the United States over the last five years. I can assure you that the ability to earn equity is a major motivator for passion and commitment about the business.

In the services business, you really do have one asset, and that's your people. If you're lucky, they give you two weeks notice. No matter how well things are going, there are competitors out there who will try to hire away your best people, which is a huge risk in this business. The more positive and passionate they are about your (their) vision, their belief in you as a leader, and the more they have at stake (equity), the more likely you are to retain them.

Executing the Plan

You now have the vision, the plan, and the people. It is now time to start executing.

The real challenge in today's market is finding salespeople who can get doors open. Unfortunately, the '90s, particularly in the information

133

technology services business, were a wonderful time. It was a wonderful time because we were living in a false economy. Everybody thought everything was great, that business was going to continue growing, and that the stock market was going to go crazy. It turned out that we didn't really have salespeople but order takers instead. That was a much different environment than it is today. You have to have people who are dedicated to getting doors open. They have to be able to handle rejection because there is going to be a lot of it. Once you get in front of the client, you have to have a good story to tell, and you have to be able to show the client how you want to get involved in helping them solve their business problems. And you have to have somebody in front of the client that is credible at telling your story. Your people who are working for you have to see the vision and they have to have the passion and commitment for the business.

Then, when you get your first client, you had better do a good job. If you do a good job, you will use that first client as a reference – the most valuable kind. Getting that first client is one of the most difficult things about starting a new business. You have to have clients who are willing to trust you based on what you've told them, or based on what you've done for them in the past with a previous employer. Once you get a success under your belt, it's easier to close additional business. References are incredibly important in most businesses, which says that customer service is the most important thing. If you irritate clients and you don't do a good job for them, you're obviously not going to be able to use them as a reference.

Customer service is more important today than it was three or four years ago. At that time it wasn't a big issue in our business – if you had quality resources that you could provide to the client, you had business almost no matter how you treated them, because they were so desperate to get good people to help them with their projects. Today, it's a whole different ballgame. There are many people out there who are willing to

ESTABLISHING THE NEED

work for a lot less money than they have in the past. It's one of those things of which you have to be very cognizant. You also have to be more understanding of the demands upon the customer in trying to provide them with solutions to their problems. In the current environment, managers are under the gun to increase revenues and decrease costs. They will not acquire products or services if they do not provide a short-term return on their investment.

The biggest thing to be prepared for in the execution phase of your business is change. In today's environment, you will constantly be faced with change. Things are not going to happen as you had planned. We are living in a world economy, and we have to understand that. This affects all businesses. No longer are we affected only by what we do in this country. In our Industry, offshore services being provided by India, China, and the Philippines are going to play a major role in changing our industry. We have to be prepared to deal with that. The way to deal with that is to provide services that the offshore companies can't provide. In fact, we may very well get involved in providing offshore services to our clients where it is appropriate to do so.

In the '90s, an awful lot of clients that we served were doing Y2K work and using that as a convenient reason for replacing a lot of software and going with new technology. Unfortunately, that's not the right way to make a decision. Clients have to focus on: what kind of problem they are trying to solve; what is it going to cost; and what is the expected return. This is what the clients are going through today. It's something that we have to help them do. No matter what business you are in, you have to add value to your customer. You have to help them cut costs or add profitable revenue. That is the name of the game today and hopefully will remain long into the future.

One of the things I do to help position the company to thrive on change is to try to get people to think creatively about the business. We try to do

135

INSIDE THE MINDS

this with our business development managers who are out in front of the clients and with our consultants who are out there on a daily basis. We want them to look for opportunities where we can come in and provide client valued services. If we are successful at this, the clients will continue to use us, and hopefully say good things about us to prospective clients.

Entrepreneurs are, by nature, risk takers. The biggest risk that you take is starting the business up front. There's always a risk associated with that. Once the business is started and running, you have to be able to look at changes that are necessary as a potential risk and say, "I believe very strongly and think that this is a change that we need to make in the business." You have to be prepared, if it doesn't work, to make whatever changes are necessary to get back on track. You have to be in a financial position to be able to take risk. Can you survive if the change does not work? You do have to take risk, because without risk, the business will not grow.

In a service business it's a little easier because we don't have the tremendous capital expenditures that are required in a manufacturing or process business. There are no big plants to build and no new equipment to buy, and no distribution centers or distribution center systems necessary to get our products to the marketplace. In that sense, it is certainly easier in the services business. If we decide to add a new service and hire people who are skilled in that particular service area, we must be able to deal with reality. If the new service is not successful, we have to step up and realize that it is not working. We have to make changes or cut our losses by getting rid of the people that we put in place to try to be successful in the new service.

It is important as your company grows to be able to recognize the strengths and weaknesses of the people in your organization, including yourself. The larger you become, the more details there are too deal with and the scope of the jobs will change. Make sure you have the right people in the right jobs, and do not be afraid to confront this issue, as it will be critical to your continuing success.

My final thought on execution is communication. If you want your people to keep their passion and commitment to your vision, you must keep them informed as to what is going on. This includes both good and bad news. You are kidding yourself if you think you can hide bad news from your employees. They want to hear this news from you and not someone else. They want to know what your plan is to fix whatever the problem is and, more than likely, will want to be involved in developing the solution. If the news is good, give your employees the credit. That is probably where it belongs!

Your Personal Life

There probably isn't any entrepreneur who can say that it doesn't bother them when they lose business. When we lose a deal, it bothers me today, after twenty years in business, just as much as it did at the beginning. However, it is not something that I will lose sleep over. One of the things I told myself when I started this business was that if I ended up losing a night's sleep, then I had better go find something else to do. When I am at work, I am focused on work. When I leave work (sometimes very late), I turn it off. I think it is very important that you do that, because you really need a balance between work and personal life. In the early days of a new business, you'll be spending a lot more time at work. Some people choose to take that work home with them. I made the decision very early on that work belonged at work and personal life belonged at home.

For me, the most rewarding aspect of my entrepreneurial career has been going out there with a new idea, getting out in front of people and talking about it, watching the thing come to fruition, and reaching that point where you realize profits – those are the greatest joys. When you grow the company beyond that you realize that the bigger the business gets, the more things you have to attend to. You need to be able to recognize your strengths and weaknesses and make the necessary adjustments. The bigger you get, the more administration, rules and regulations you have to deal with. To me, personally, this takes a lot of fun out of the business. It's one of the reasons I brought in a president and chief operating officer so that I could spend my time out with our employees and with our clients. That, to me, is where the fun is in the business. And I am not as good at the day-to-day details of running a business, as I should be.

Conclusion

To be entrepreneurial, you really have to be a visionary. You have to be careful not to take your eye off of the objective and the vision, and relax when you have achieved your first success. It is easy to get the feeling "Wow! I'm really good." Be Careful! You really have to concentrate on keeping your eye on the long-term objective, and realize that there will be highs and lows. Don't relax. It takes a lot of hard work and long hours, particularly up front, to be successful in starting a business. Another one of Vince Lombardi's quotes that I am fond of is: "It is easy to have faith in yourself and have discipline when you are a winner, when you're number one. What you've got to have is faith and discipline when you're not yet a winner."

Too many people make starting a business a complex thing. I don't think that it has to be that complex, and most people are capable of starting their own successful business. You have to be willing to take the risks and make the sacrifices necessary. You need to have the attitude that this is something that you will be successful at, make money at, and accomplish something for the good. The thing that is more important to

ESTABLISHING THE NEED

me than anything else is that my people respect me for what I have done and continue to do. I think I have been successful at that. The people in our organization know that I care about them.

Most importantly, you have to have a passion and commitment for your idea and your vision, and you must have to have a willingness to share your success with those who help you succeed. That's something you need to think about and plan for from the very beginning.

The Golden Rules of Starting and Running a Successful Business

Knowledge of the Industry
A Vision of Where You are Trying to Go
A Passion for What You are Doing
A Commitment to Success
A Willingness to Share That Success with Those That Helped You Achieve It

Dave Cassell is a graduate of the University of Kansas with a B. A. Degree in Personnel Management. He spent fifteen years with IBM's Data Processing Division marketing hardware, software, and services. He achieved 10 hundred percent clubs in ten years on quota and was the top new business salesman in 1979.

Dave left IBM in January of 1982 to start a contract/consulting company. Pro-Access, Access to Professionals, grew to over 10 million dollars in revenue in 1989, and, in 1990, became a part of the RCG International family of consulting companies. Dave served as President of RCG Pro-Access and a Senior Vice President and Director of RCG International. In 1996, Dave took responsibility for Corporate Planning and Business Development at the corporate level.

After leaving RCG in early 1997, Dave began working on a new paradigm for the Information Technology Services Industry and started his new company, Consultants' Choice, Inc., in September of 1997. With revenues of 11.1 million dollars in 1999, the University of Houston and the Houston Business Journal recognized Consultants' Choice, Inc. as the fastest growing privately held high tech company in Houston from 1997 to 1999 and the second fastest growing company in any industry. In 2001, the University of Houston, Bauer College of Business Center for Entrepreneurship and Innovation recognized Consultants' Choice as one of the three companies in Houston with the greatest potential for growth. Recently, Consultants' Choice was recognized by Inc. Magazine as the 23rd fastest growing company in the United States over the last five years.

Dave has been active in both community and professional organizations, including Rotary International, Boy Scouts of America, and the Independent Computer Consultants Association (ICCA). He was a founder of the National Association of Computer Consultant Businesses (NACCB) and is a past President and Chairman of that Organization. He was also a founder, Board Member, and Fund Raising Chair for the Open Door Education Foundation (ODEF).

The Importance of Validating Your Business

Bob Lokken
ProClarity Corporation
President & CEO

Setting Out

An entrepreneur must start their company with the idea that they're going create some value in the world, in other words to provide some product or service that solves some problem for people. That problem might be as serious as providing a cure for cancer, or as light as providing a fun place for people to have lunch. Even though there are many problems in the world, not all of them are worth solving. Your potential customers might in fact have the problem you seek to address; they may or may not even acknowledge that it is, in fact, a problem, but it's not high enough on their priority list that they would actually spend any money to solve the issue.

There are many critical issues that are involved in creating a business. Perhaps the most critical is that you develop a sense of the stages that most new businesses must go through before they become viable and successful enterprises. Like a baby that must develop from a infant, to a child, an adolescent, and then finally an adult – the evolution of the business must follow a developmental process. The importance in understanding these stages comes from the fact that most start-ups fail when the entrepreneur is either not aware or foolishly attempts to skip stages in the process. Failure to understand the conceptual stages and plan accordingly usually not only slows down the development of the business, but additionally can create serious problems, such as misestimating cash requirements and/or running out of cash – which is what kills most start-ups.

There are five stages a new business needs to plan on developing through:

Conception – "You can not create what you can not conceive." This stage is the "idea and planning" stage where ideas are created, sorted through, business concepts flushed out, business plans drafted, etc.

THE IMPORTANCE OF VALIDATING YOUR BUSINESS

Creation –This is the stage where the product/service is created, faculties established, marketing and sales materials created, etc.

Validation – This stage is the least understood, most skipped, and far and away provides the most significant source of problems when skipped. Frustration and failure typically awaits those who foolishly ignore this critical stage. When an endeavor fails to "get off the ground" this stage is typically the stopping point.

Replication –This stage is where you discover if your first few customers/successes were a fluke, or if the value proposition and economic exchange at the core of the business can be reliably repeated.

Scaling – This stage is where the founding team figures out how to economically scale the business operations beyond their personal day-to-day supervision. It consists of the hiring of more people, building training programs, systems, processes, and infrastructure that enable the business to scale-up its operations. This stage may not be of interest to some entrepreneur if their goal is to create a small, personal business. For those that wish to scale the business beyond that point, this stage is where repeatable and reliable systems and processes replace the personal heroics, drive, and often sheer brute force of the founders.

It is very difficult to skip steps one or two given that without them, you do not even have something to sell. Many business books and schools stress the business planning stages and point out the pitfalls of shortchanging or not thoroughly planning the start up. While this is very true, it is useful to understand that it is in fact the failure to plan for stage three – validation – that is where most fall down.

Many an eager entrepreneur pour heart and soul into their "perfect" business plan, only to later painfully learn that a plan is not a business. Plans are like maps that allow us to plot how we are going to get to our desired destination. But beware, the map is not the terrain. What's more, the entrepreneurial dilemma is that our maps are drawn up detailing terrain that has often not ever been traveled. Thus, the entrepreneurial

143

map is a guesstimate of the terrain to be crossed and the obstacles that must be navigated.

Because the map was drawn up prior to actually being experienced – the obstacles and paths on the map are actually our assumptions. The validation stage is critical as it is where the start-up first experiences the real terrain the business must cross. The most important first step is to validate the assumptions. In order to successfully reach our destination, the real terrain (obstacles and opportunities) must be discovered. The original map (our first business plan) may require small adjustments, or it may require major changes, in order to accurately address the real issues.

From a tactical perspective, cash flow is the most important thing to a start-up business. Cash is the fuel we use to travel across the terrain to our destination. If you run out of cash, it is effectively like running out of gas and being stranded – all the other ideas and execution plans don't matter much anymore. This is where the importance of validation comes in. If you do not validate your plan, you are likely to continue to act on bad assumptions and thus yield poor or no results. As the business struggles to sell it products/services, the cash is being used up, and obviously, it is eventually gone – and so is the business. It is critical that the validation stage be planned on and executed as fast as possible.

Statistics show that a large majority of start-ups fail, and the overwhelming, most often stated reason is that the endeavor "ran out of cash". In my personal experiences these studies are misleading as people imply that with more cash the business would have worked. Running out of cash is a symptom of the problem, not the root problem. The core problem is typically that the business did not quickly enough validate and adjust their plans/offerings, and thus depleted all their cash pursuing a plan that would have never been economically feasible, regardless of the money spent.

144

THE IMPORTANCE OF VALIDATING YOUR BUSINESS

How do you validate your business plan? You must focus on getting some paying customers as early as possible. Why paying customers? Because what you are trying to validate is that your value proposition is economically feasible. You are not trying to validate that people "like" what you offer, or that they are "very interested". There is a big difference between liking something and being willing to pay the money you need to charge them to make the operation variable. There are many things that you learn when you ask people to buy your product or service that you won't learn sitting around running a spreadsheet or writing a business plan.

Failure to validate a viable economic value proposition and business model was rampant in the wild dot-com bubble era. It is vital to your survival that you internalize that the purpose of the business is to generate revenues and profits, not to spend money. Far too many people mistake spending money with generating results. Money is spent to generate a profit. You may be losing money in the early days, and that is because you are investing in creating the offer and validating the plan. If you blindly execute and fail to get to a valid model, then you will likely continue to lose money until it is gone. This is hard stuff. It's easy to put together a marketing plan and start buying advertising and so on, but that's not the point of the business. The sooner you validate the model that will actually work, you can then move on to the next stage – replicating the model.

A quick note – those early customers are important for a second reason. One of the most difficult things start-ups often face is a lack of credibility. Your early credibility is not going to come from the fact that you are a household name, or that you are listed on the New York Stock Exchange. Your early credibility is going to come from being able to say, "I have solved this problem for customers very similar to you, and they have been very successful with this." So having customers ASAP that have been successful with your product or service, or that have a successful experience with your business, are critical reference points in credibility. And with a start-up, credibility is everything.

Replicating the value proposition is what you focus on after the proposition has been validated. A very common mistake and a way to waste a lot of money is to skip validation and start replicating a value proposition that does not work economically. Actually, replication is really the second phase of validation. Initially validation is about proving things out once or twice and getting those first happy customers. The replication stage is where you find out if this value proposition is going to sell over and over again. More specifically, this is where you find out what it is going to take to sell it over and over again. Once the replication stage is figured out, the business is now viable, and baring some specific planned investment, it should be running at a profit. If the business is replicating it sales and is still losing money (again, assuming no significant new investment is being made), then the replication stage is not yet complete, as the point is to get to an economically viable value proposition.

How much money you need really, typically, depends on what you're going to do – more specifically, how much time and money is needed to go through the stages from conception, to creation, to validation, to then building a replicable model? For example, the business you're starting requires that you go into some sort of product development that drives capital requirements because until you have something to sell, you're not going to have any revenue. (I'm in high tech, and most start-ups start by developing a product, and it can take anywhere from six months to six years before they can start selling it.) So there's a certain amount of upfront investment to get to the point where you have something to sell, and you know how to sell it, that should dictate how much capital you need. A common mistake, especially with venture capital-funded start-ups, is that they get money and then they try to scale the business when they haven't validated their business plan yet. They write the business

146

THE IMPORTANCE OF VALIDATING YOUR BUSINESS

plan, they fund the business plan, and then they go off and execute as if it's actually going to work. That is a very expensive way to validate your business plan. If you hire 16 sales reps before you have figured out how to make one sales rep productive, that consumes a lot of money.

Don't forget or be naive – do you have enough money to go out and test the concept, come back, make some changes, and then go out and try again? Because if you only have enough money to get up to bat once, so to speak, you are basically betting the entire company on the hope that the first plan that you have is right on the money. And plans are wrong more often than they're right. It may be a good business plan, but there are usually some key assumptions that you made that don't pan out and that need to be adjusted before you get a business model that actually works. You have to recognize, for example, when you're doing your financial capital requirements planning that when you take this to market, you're not going to suddenly have 1,000 customers the next month paying you $100,000 each. It's not going to work that way. You're going to build 1-2-3, and you're going to spend several months getting the mix right before you're ready to start landing a lot of customers.

Focus

Another key thing to remember is that you need to commit the company to a single direction, and put every ounce of energy into doing one thing better than anybody on the planet. So rather than trying to do 17 things reasonably well, we decided to do one thing and be world-class at it. That's a hard strategy to maintain because when you start getting customers, they start saying, "Why don't you have this capability? You do a really good job in this – could you add this?" Sometimes you get thrown out of deals because you don't do enough things. But you have to pick your battles. As an entrepreneur, you have to win most of the battles

147

you get in, so it's critical that you pick the right battles. You can't pick six battles – you can't afford to lose five times. So you pick one battle, and then you do everything humanly possible to win that battle.

Major Pitfalls

Misguided Focus
As mentioned before - one of the major pitfalls entrepreneurs face is believing in the business plan too much. They have so much personal effort involved that they become zealots about the business plan rather than zealots about success. The focus must be reaching the goal, not following the plan. It's kind of like the old definition of insanity: continuing to do the same thing over and over again and expecting a different outcome. If the plan is not getting you closer to the goal, change the plan.

If the entrepreneurs or the people who start the business came from big companies and if that's their only work experience, they tend to fall into the trap of confusing what businesses do with what makes businesses successful. I know start-ups that put in a day care center before they opened their doors because successful companies have day care centers or they have workout rooms. That's confusing something that is the result of success with something that causes success because no company got successful by having day care at the office. After you are successful, then you can afford to put in a day care center.

If people who are starting companies don't get that, they tend to be in big trouble because they focus on the appearance of being in business rather than actually being in business. They spend money on furniture and nice business cards and great web sites and great logos and on getting the right dot-com name. And what they forget is that, fundamentally, the job of the business is not spending that money, it's actually making money,

THE IMPORTANCE OF VALIDATING YOUR BUSINESS

and that's where all the focus should be in the early stages. Because it's hard, if you don't focus on it, it's not going to happen by accident.

Blindness

I've seen many people put together an initial business plan, take a run at the marketplace with that, and then come back and say, "We haven't had success yet." Remember the goal of validation is feedback. Whenever you're engaged with the market, you are always getting results; they may not be the result you were looking for, but you either choose to pay attention to them or not. Be careful to not dismiss bad results too early. Saying, "Oh, that customer didn't really understand what we were doing, we need to find someone else" may be the proper course of action, but perhaps they are telling you something. You have to be willing to engage with the market, and then be open to learning what that is telling you about your concept. Blindness is refusing to see what the results are or coloring the results with pre-conceived basis.

Running Out Of Cash and Spending

Sometime running out of cash is a symptom of another problem; sometimes you just plain run out of cash before your can stand on your own two feet. In either case, it is usually deadly or you end up liquidating most or all of the equity for a fraction of the value you hoped to create.

Mistaking Cause and Effect

It seems that you can nearly always tell a start-up that is not going to make it very early on by watching how the founders spend the money. If the company has expensive offices, lots of perks, nice hotels, first class flights, etc., then they are not spending their capital in the right places, and it is a sure bet they are going to run out. Nice things are fine (if you like that stuff) but, as a general rule, you should always pay for that stuff only out of profits – thus, if the company is not making a profit, don't spend money on anything that does not add to your ability to build sales. Once again, people sometimes confuse themselves; they see successful

INSIDE THE MINDS

companies have nice office, day cares, etc., but they fail to understand those things are the results of being successful, not the cause of the success.

Losing Site of the Goal
Small companies should be opportunistic and nimble – it is a core advantage they have over bigger rivals. But you need to maintain some sense of focus on the ultimate goal and not get distracted and pulled in too many directions.

Giving Up Speed
One of the huge advantages a small company has over a big company is speed, and it's really foolish to give that advantage away. With big companies – by the time you do the business planning model with 150 people involved and everybody has to collaborate on it, and everybody comes to agreement, then you have to go out and deploy it to 15,000 people – it takes a year and a half by the time you get the entire team executing on the business plan. A small company can do that in a weekend. But if you refuse to revise and adjust your business plan based on the opportunities you're seeing in the marketplace, or based on the results you're having, then although you're small and therefore nimble, you're not being nimble – you're being static. You have to be opportunistic in a small company because you can't just walk in and overpower marketplaces. You go to market, and you say, "This isn't working out, but if we made this small change, this customer would buy it." Then you start to ask yourself, "Is that the only customer who would want that, or is that actually the true niche that we're going to fill?"

Measuring Progress and Success

You have to know where you're going or where you're trying to go. If you're getting feedback, you want to know if that feedback means you're

THE IMPORTANCE OF VALIDATING YOUR BUSINESS

moving closer to success or farther away. It takes two data points. One is that you have to have a plan, so you know specifically what you're trying to achieve, and you can get everybody on the team lined up on the plan to be executed. But then you have to constantly monitor results to see if you are achieving what you want to achieve, and if not, why not? And then you make the appropriate adjustments.

To measure whether you're succeeding or not, you simply ask whether you're achieving the goal you set out to achieve. If you set out to build a $100 million company, how are you doing? If you set out to have a restaurant chain with five restaurants, do you have five yet? You set out with a goal, and you measure success based on how well you are achieving that goal. Some people's goals might be wrapped up in money. Some people might start a business because they want to have an impact on society, and they think the business can do that. Some people just want a yacht. Some people want to run their own business, under the mistaken impression that when you're in charge, you have complete control over your day. I find that the bigger we get, the less control I have over my day, because people need things from you. You need to focus on your original goal and whether you are achieving that or not. That is why it's important to have a plan. If you don't have a plan, how do you know whether you're being successful or not? The long hours start to make you feel like a hamster on one of those little wheels after a while, unless you can see that you're making progress.

Not Acknowledging or Planning for Risks

The most important part of taking risks is just keeping your eyes wide open. If you believe in what you're doing but you're also realistic enough to know that your business plan has not been validated yet – you don't know if it's actually going to work that way or if it's going to have to change by 10 percent or by 75 percent before you get something that's

151

commercially viable – then you've got your eyes wide open and you can see the risks coming, and you can mitigate them and deal with them. Risk becomes unbearable when it blindsides you – when you either don't see it or you refuse to see it. With entrepreneurs, a lot of them refuse to see it. They're so passionate about what they do and they're so convinced that what they're doing is right that they refuse to accept external feedback, and they refuse to acknowledge the risk that exists in what they're doing. And that's the biggest risk of all. As long as you know the risks you're taking, then you can deal with them accordingly. Blind risk is the real problem.

The CEO of the start-up I worked for right out of college once told me that the difference between a successful businessman and an unsuccessful businessman was that a successful businessman was right 51 percent of the time and wrong 49 percent of the time, and the unsuccessful businessman had those two numbers reversed. That always stuck with me because you can't be too arrogant. You have to admit when you've made a mistake, or you never learn. That was a key observation because it put things in perspective. When people lose, it's not because they're stupid – it's because they made a couple of wrong critical decisions. And when people win, it's not that they didn't make any mistakes – it's that they had more successes than mistakes. As an entrepreneur, you're creating new things, by definition, so you're going to make some mistakes. The key is that you recognize quickly when you've made a mistake and correct it. If you think you get the answer right 90 percent of the time, I'll guarantee you're going to fail as an entrepreneur. There are multiple approaches that will work and dozens and dozens of ways that won't. You have to make a decision and execute it with focus, and then, if it's the wrong decision, change it. Don't get proud or caught up in it; just change it. Don't fall in love with your business plan; pay attention to whether you're being successful or not, and then adapt and adjust.

The Curse of Too Much Capital

Over funding a start-up is often much more deadly than under funding a start-up. When you have a lot of money, people tend to focus their attention on spending that money, but spending money doesn't necessarily mean getting customers or making revenue. The classic example would be buying an advertisement on the Super Bowl for a product that nobody understands. Advertisement is about exposure, but if people don't even understand what you do, exposure is not going to help much. Some products and services are easily understood with little explanation. Other things that entrepreneurs dream up require that customers be educated as to what it is and why they should buy it from you.

It has been documented time and time again: If you have too many resources, people focus on how they're going to use their resources rather than on how they're going to be successful. So if they measure success as burning through all their capital, then they are successful, but, typically, that is not how businesses are measured. The goal is not to spend money – it's to make money. If you don't have a whole lot of resources, you have to focus on the critical few things that you have to do and do well. If you have a lot of money, you don't ever have to have the focus discussion. And if you don't focus as a small company, you're history. You're just dead. Because a big company is like an army moving across Europe, whereas an entrepreneurial company is like five guys in a little team trying to go in and create a foothold somewhere. You can't take five people and put one every mile. They have to work together closely as a team, and they have to have a focal point. They can't be scattered across 100 miles of front, so to speak. You have to have everybody focus.

If you don't have a lot of money, people have to be creative, and they have to focus. If you have a lot of money, people just tend to fall into the mode of spending money. During the dot-com era, I saw start-up after start-up get a lot of money from venture capitalists, and then they would immediately come back and spend a month and a half picking out new office furniture – "Hey, we've got to renovate the office, we need state-of-the-art telecommunications equipment, we've got to put in this big web center, and we need all this top-of-the-line equipment because we're going to have this incredibly big business." But all that not only costs money, it costs time. And it's time that you're not spending focused on learning who your customers are, how you are going to add value to your customers, and how you are going to get paid for what you do.

I've seen people whose idea was – and this was classic in the dot-com era – to create paying customers by giving away their product to a million people. That's an interesting way to get one million customers, but if they didn't pay anything, what was the point? That's fine as long as there is a point, but a lot of times people get confused and they think the point is getting the million customers that don't pay you anything – but that doesn't pay the bills. You're supposed to be making money, not spending it. This was really common in the dot-com era because people were throwing so much money at start-ups. And the money was actually causing their failure, for the most part, in my opinion. Because these companies had so much money, they went off and chased things. They never validated anything – they just scaled it. If you've got something that doesn't work and you scale it, it just creates that much bigger of an explosion when it blows up. So rather than starting small and iterating your process until you figure it out and then scaling it, people were just writing it down in a business plan, getting the money, and then scaling it, before they'd ever figured out whether it would actually work. And that model just fundamentally does not work. It might work on occasion, but it's more like a lightening-strike type of a model rather than a systematic process of building value in a company.

THE IMPORTANCE OF VALIDATING YOUR BUSINESS

The curse of too much capital is a major pitfall. Most entrepreneurs would think it's the curse of not enough capital. Many companies go out because they run out of money; however, if you fail because you run out of money, it may be because you ran out of money, or it may be because what you did was never going to work – and if we had doubled the money, you would have just gone twice as long before you failed. It's easy to confuse the cause and effect relationships here. One reason you run out of money is because the business model you're executing fundamentally doesn't work. But I've never met an entrepreneur who would say that. I've met experienced entrepreneurs who would admit that, but I've never met somebody who has tried it once and failed who would ever admit that. They would say, "Well, we ran out of money." If it wasn't going to work, then regardless of the amount of money put in, you're going to run out of that, too.

Sometimes good companies actually do run out of money, typically because of a miscalculation of time to get a replicable model, or some risks they take don't pan out. But given that it is the management's job to make sure you don't run out of money, if you run out of money, you failed, and you need to accept that responsibility. You failed to get financing, you failed to get customers – whatever. You failed.

Venture Capitalists aren't really spending their money now, but for quite a few years there were people who were getting a lot of start-up money, and then they were going out and spending it, only to find out after the money was gone that they didn't have any customers and they didn't have any revenue. That led to massive layoffs and a massive stock implosion if the company had already gone public. Money is good and money is bad, just like everything else. Not having enough is bad; having too much is also bad. People don't recognize that.

Employing the Network

Networking is critical in two areas for a start-up. One is in getting your first customers, because if you have no existing customers and no credibility, it's very hard to get someone in the door, to sign up for what you're offering. You don't have a lot of credibility. People who know you personally can say, "I'm not really sure about the product here, but this guy is really smart, and I've seen him do some amazing things in the past, and I think we should at least hear him out." Networks will get you an audience; they won't ever sell the deal for you. Sometimes they do, but those are not the customers you want because they're not telling you whether what you're doing is of value – they're just telling you that what you have is something that they bought because you're their brother-in-law. And that can be a very, very deceiving thing. You have to find people who would actually buy the product or service for what the value is that you are actually intending to provide, or you will run out of contacts pretty quickly. So networking is very important to get your foot in the door with some initial customers.

It is also extremely important in raising money. Having a personal introduction is especially critical if you're going after professional money or angel investors. Those people get bombarded with business plans in the mail all day long, and your chances of actually getting an audience with a venture capitalist go up about 1,000 percent if you actually know somebody at the firm. At least, initially, this establishes a degree of credibility.

When you are an entrepreneurial company or a seedling company, the only thing you have is your personal credibility and the skills of the initial founders. That's the only asset you have. You have a business plan, but the business plan is just a piece of paper. If somebody doesn't execute it, then it doesn't matter how brilliant the plan was – if it's not executed, it's not going to work. And the people who put together the

THE IMPORTANCE OF VALIDATING YOUR BUSINESS

business plan and adjust it and tweak it are the initial founding partners. So you don't have a product that anybody has experience with, but you have people with experience. That's the network. And that is what you need to leverage. Your only point of credibility as a small company is the management team itself, so networking for capital and networking for early customer contacts are critical.

The Management Team and Leadership

Early on, the management team is a group of people who are going to spend a significant amount of time together. Not all of those times are going to be good times, so one of the critical aspects is that you find people who have a shared set of goals. If you and I have a shared set of goals, when particular bumps in the road come up and we run into problems, we can work through those because, at the end of the day, we're both trying to achieve the same thing. But if my goal is to run the company up and then be acquired after two years and put a couple million dollars in my pocket, and your goal is to build the company over the next 20 years, it's not going to work. You have a different set of goals, and that influences the decisions that you make every minute of every day. You make decisions differently if you are shooting for one outcome rather than another. So I think it is critical that you get people who can work together, who trust each other, and who have shared goals. Because you're going to be spending a lot of time together, and if you don't trust each other, or if you have a different set of goals, it will all fall apart.

My personal management style is probably much more collaborative and delegate than that of a typical entrepreneur. I believe that one of the key things any manager can do – but it's especially important if you are the CEO of a company – is to be really good at self-assessment. You must be really brutally honest about "here's what I'm good at, and here's what

157

INSIDE THE MINDS

I'm really bad at." Then you have to build out a management team.
You've heard people in the self-help world say, "You need to identify
your weaknesses and then work on those." No, you don't. Not when
you're starting a company. What you need to do is identify your
strengths and stick to them. You need to identify your weaknesses and
hire people who complement those weaknesses. And then you need to
basically let them run. I have a vice president of marketing; if it's a
marketing issue, it's his decision, not mine. I have a CFO; if it's a
financial decision, it's his decision, not mine. Now, ultimately, I have
veto rights, but I trust those people because they know their specific
disciplines better than I do. And if I didn't trust them to know more
about it than I do, then there would be no reason to have them here. If
they're just going to do what you tell them to do, you can hire an
administrative assistant to do that. You need to surround yourself with
people who offset your weaknesses, and then you need to trust them.

In today's business environment, especially in a knowledge worker
business, the number one attribute essential to good leadership (which
will probably surprise people) is the ability to listen. The reason is that
people – this is not a military analogy – have a choice whether they want
to follow you or not. Not many very smart people will follow you if you
think so little of them that you won't even listen to what they have to say.
People get hung up on this sometimes, because they think that if they
listen to somebody, then they have to do what they say. To me, those are
two completely different things.

First, you have to listen, and you have to have knowledge – and a passion
for where you're going. You have to have some kind of unique
knowledge to provide leadership, and you have to have passion for your
vision, because if you are not passionate about it, they're never going to
be passionate about it. You want people to be excited about where
they're going – and that passion has to start with you. Sometimes leaders
get reserved and tentative, and then they are confused when their people

158

THE IMPORTANCE OF VALIDATING YOUR BUSINESS

are reserved and tentative. If you are passionate about your vision, then others can be passionate about it.

The worst part about being a leader is when you figure out that everybody expects you to have all the answers, but in this particular situation you have no clue. That's the worst part about being a leader: People look to you to know what the right thing is to do all the time – not all the time, but much of the time – and sometimes they do it in an area in which you simply have no idea what the right thing to do is. The way I deal with that is just by being completely honest with people. I say, "You know, I don't have a clue. There are a lot of problems here; there are a lot of conflicting answers here. I think we should try this, but I don't really know." I think if you just admit what you don't know, people will respect that. And they'll contribute. But it's hard when you're a leader, because everybody expects you to have all the answers.

The Entrepreneurial Mindset

Entrepreneurs are always looking for broken things so they can fix them. They're always looking to fix something or do something better. Fundamentally, most entrepreneurs I've met who are successful always want to do something better. Whatever they've decided – whether they own a restaurant or they started a software company or a media company – they've said, "I can service that market better. I can offer a better product or service for this set of customers than anybody else." Given that that is a base characteristic, they're not really satisfied with the status quo.

That is why they're often very disruptive in big companies. You can't have somebody who is constantly trying to change things because it took you 18 months to roll out the last change. You can't have people constantly ripping the system down. The job of managers in big

159

companies is to perpetuate the system and get consistent, repeatable output from the system. Entrepreneurs like to tear systems down and rebuild them in a different way. That's their nature. They want to be creative about things. They always want to say, "Yeah, that works, but it could work better. Let's go build that. It could work better." That is why it is far more the exception than the rule when an entrepreneur is successful through multiple stages of a company's life. When it becomes about repetition and building systems that create a repeatable output, most entrepreneurs don't fit into the business model very well. So they typically get the company to a certain level and then they hand it off to somebody else. There are certain people who are not entrepreneurial but who are very much about managing, and they just want to make sure that everything gets done. They want to set up systems and processes so that everything gets done the way it's supposed to get done. And most entrepreneurs would find that very constrictive. They like the fact that they don't know what they're going to do when they get into the office every day.

When you're a seed company, before you've got customers, you're not worried about growth; you're worried about if you can actually sell whatever you've got. The entrepreneur's job at that point should be actually trying to sell it. You should be the person out trying to convince people to do this – it is your vision, you know it best, you have the most passion for the value you add. .

The second phase in a company's life is, after you've got something to sell, you've sold it a few times, and you know you can sell it, now how do you grow it? In that phase, one of the important shifts is moving from doing it yourself to building a company that can do it. Many entrepreneurs get tripped up in that particular area – they're really good at selling it, but they can never hire anybody who can sell it. There's a limit to how many deals you can personally close in a quarter, so at some point, pretty early on, growth is about scaling the business. You know

THE IMPORTANCE OF VALIDATING YOUR BUSINESS

you can sell it, but that's no longer the question. The question is, if you're going to grow, you've got to be able to hire four people in the next six months, and they've got to be able to sell it. So it becomes more about building the machine rather than running the machine. Rather than actually engaging with customers, you have to shift into the hiring process and the training process.

For me – and I think this is probably true for most pure entrepreneurs – there never really is an "aha" moment. As soon as you get to some milestone that you set for yourself, you're almost immediately asking what's next. What do you have to do to get to the next level? Most entrepreneurs I know, if their first goal was doing $1 million a year, when they hit that, they have a beer, and then they say, "Wouldn't it be cool if we could do $1 million a month? What would we have to do to do that? How many customers would we have to see? How many people would we have to hire? Do we need to expand the building?" And they start working on the next thing they're going to build. I don't personally ever sit back and say, "Wow! Look what I built," because I'm always consumed by "What am I building?" I call this attribute in people "playing down the field" – most highly motivated, high achievers have this trait.

Identifying Opportunities

If you are going to enter large national and international markets, you need some sort of disruption in the marketplace. If everybody is happy with the current vendors, there will be no room for a new vendor to come in. So there must be some disruptive force, such as a changing technology or a changing market space where some new things are happening that the old companies aren't addressing very well. Those are the opportunities you're trying to thrive on. You're looking for those

INSIDE THE MINDS

gaps where customers' needs have diverged from the offerings of the current companies they're doing business with.

For example, back in the early days, Ford was making cars, and he was making them cheap, and everybody thought that was fantastic. Somebody asked him one day, "What if we want a different color?" And Ford said, "You can have any color you want as long as it's black." He didn't care about color; what he cared about was making a cheap, reliable vehicle that he could mass-produce and sell for cheap. Or, say, people decided that there was more to a car than reliability, and now colors and chrome wheels and all these other things started to be important. That type of situation creates opportunities in the market because if the existing vendors don't respond for whatever reason to the changing market – sometimes they can't respond, because the nature of the change makes it hard for them to respond – those are the opportunities that entrepreneurial companies jump in on.

Microsoft was launched when computers started weighing less than 20 pounds – something that could sit on your desktop rather than something that took up a large room. There was new technology that created a disruption; the disruption was an opportunity for a small company to get in and thrive. Microsoft capitalized on the microchip market long before any of the big computer companies could even fathom responding to it, because it was just too small of a market for them to worry about. But by the time that it was a big enough market for them to worry about, Microsoft had already established itself and had gotten the toehold it needed to compete with bigger companies.

As a small company, you're looking for those disruptions. You're looking for a situation in which customers are dissatisfied because of something that has changed, and they are going to be open to talking to a small, unknown vendor – somebody they have never heard of – to solve the problem. You're constantly looking for this opportunity. You identify

162

THE IMPORTANCE OF VALIDATING YOUR BUSINESS

the market you're going to play in, and then you just stay all over the market so you understand all the dynamics of what's going on and you can see when new opportunities are emerging. As a small company you can change your plans very quickly, so you can be very opportunistic. You can respond to a change in the market.

With more than 15 years of hands-on experience in the software industry, Bob Lokken provides the critical insight that has successfully guided ProClarity through pitfalls which often prove fatal to companies supported by less experienced leadership. He has won numerous industry awards, holds several database technology patents and has spoken at numerous conferences on database technology. Prior to founding ProClarity, Bob served in many roles at Extended Systems, Incorporated (ESI) (Nasdaq-XTND), including General Manager of the company's software division, managing all Corporate Research & Development functions, and serving as Director of Information Systems. Bob holds a Bachelor of Science in Computer Science from Montana State University and has studied Operations Research and Business Administration at two different universities.

Start-Up Fundamentals

Patrick J. Martucci
United Asset Coverage, Inc.
Chairman of the Board, Chief Executive Officer

The Three Doorways To Any Market

Just about everyone, sometime during their life, gets an idea for a new product, or service. Some of those ideas are taken to the next step of creating a business, and finding a way to penetrate a market with the new product or service. While many diverse markets exist in the United States, or any other country for that matter, there are only three basic strategies, or "doorways", to gain entry to those markets. The three doorways are 1) Make a market, 2) Take a market, or 3) Change a market. Whether one is contemplating starting a business from scratch, or driving an existing organization, all business plans will take one of these three doorways, and each of the three possess very different characteristics. Once the doorway is understood and selected, all the other elements of business decisions including capital requirements, marketing strategy, competitive analysis, employee competencies, etc., will become more clear and therefore more readily defined.

"Make" a Market

In the early '80s, I had the privilege to work for a young Texas-based company that invented and was issued the patent for voicemail, which today is a familiar technology that has been accepted in both the commercial and consumer markets. At the time, however, voicemail did not exist, few understood what the thing was; my family did not understand what I did for a living, and I even believe that my grandmother thought I "delivered" the mail. In short, we were "making" a market. At its root, making a market is defined when the sale of the product or service is not at the expense of an incumbent competitor providing a similar produce or service.

The great benefit of a Make strategy is that you are offering a fresh new product, and with the absence of competition, higher margins can be achieved. The compelling product offering you propose to a prospect is one that they haven't heard before, so it is interesting and innovative. Salespeople like to sell in environments like this, and people like to work in those types of companies.

The great challenge in a Make strategy that is oftentimes underestimated is the lengthy education curve the marketplace requires to understand the benefits of this new exciting product or service. This education period can, in some cases, be years. I can tell you, firsthand, that I have heard many voicemail prospects in the '80s say, "You know, we just don't do any of that here at our company." Yet today, they all have voicemail systems in place at their companies. It simply took a number of years before the industry understood what the product was. With that said, there were early adopters who saw the benefit of voice mail and a sale was made. However, the long market education curve required the company to work from a large capital base to fund the long sales cycle.

The next doorway is the "Take" a market strategy, and this is what the majority of start-ups do. In addition to serving as CEO of UAC, I am also active in the venture capital community, and my partners and I review and consider investing in a fair number of new business plans each quarter. The vast majority of them are on a "Take strategy." Let's use the example of a long distance reseller. In this example, there is no education curve a prospect must overcome. The environment does not require a salesperson to say, "We offer a new service that once you dial certain numbers on your telephone, you can talk to someone who is located very far away." Everyone has long distance service, and everyone understands what it is. Further, everyone has an existing budget for this service.

The challenge in a Take strategy is that the differentiator tends to be price. The action you are asking the prospect to take is to switch from their current service to your service, and few prospects are willing to switch to a more expensive service than the one they have. So as long as the in-place service is meeting the needs of the prospect, a lower price will be required to win the client. In almost all cases, the Take strategy is an environment with many competitors and prospects have many choices. Over time, the product or service is viewed as a commodity, and the lowest cost provider wins the largest market share. That said, the lowest cost provider does not always win the largest market share. Staying with our long distance example, the largest long distance provider in America is still AT&T. Although hundreds of long distance competitors have been trying to "take" clients from AT&T with lower cost alternatives, the AT&T brand is powerful enough to hold the clients' loyalty. If you are in a Take strategy, you must be prepared to meet the challenge of lower price, and still overcome the brand loyalty the incumbent provider enjoys. At its root, the Take strategy is defined when one company wins a new client, and another company loses a current client.

The last doorway is the "Change" a market strategy. In a Change strategy you are not offering a new invention as in the Make strategy, and you are not offering a similar service for less as in the Take strategy. Rather, a Change strategy attempts to alter the dynamics of how a marketplace works to make it more efficient, and by creating this new changed process, value will be created in the service or product offered. An example of a Change strategy can found in today's on-line travel services. These services allow people to purchase airline tickets, hotel rooms, and other things via the Internet. While there are occasional cost savings to the consumer, interestingly enough, the price you pay for an airfare on United Airlines via the on-line service is the same price you would pay if you called United Airlines direct. However, the on-line service allows the consumer to search and view the fares and departure/arrival times of many carriers conveniently and accurately.

The consumer can also book other travel-related services such as hotels and car rentals at the same time. The key issue to note is that the price for these services are not necessarily lower than if you purchased the services direct from the supplier, but the ease of use and expanded choices provide a value the consumer did not have before the on-line service was established. In this example, the on-line travel service "changed" the way consumers buy airline tickets.

By creating this new "changed" process, they picked up one of the key benefits that exist in the Make strategy in that they created a fresh new product and still enjoy limited competition. They also picked up one of the benefits of the Take strategy in that they do not need to educate the market on the benefits of airline travel. Further, the Change strategy does not require a lower price as the differentiator.

The "Make," "Take," and "Change" doorways are the three key approaches into a marketplace, and the path you take will define the type of employees you need to hire, how large you need to be initially, the competitive forces you will face, how much capital you need to raise, and what role PR should play in the new company.

Getting Your First Customers and Building Your Internal Organization

When we started United Asset Coverage we deployed a "Change" strategy. We sought to change the way corporate America maintains its technology assets. On day one we had no customers, no history, no references, and we could not provide prospects with impressive financial reports. Since our method was a new "change" to an industry process, no clients were doing what we were asking our prospects to do. The one thing we did have was the substantial cost of a newly started company with employees in 17 cities by day one. We needed clients.

Getting your first customer is always a challenge, but that challenge can be reduced if you focus on who to call on initially. On the first day, you know that the first customer you need to secure is an early adopting customer – a prospect who, when you talk to them, asks the type of questions that are relative to the solution you are offering. If the questions they ask are: "How long have you been in business?" "How many references do you have?" "Can I see financials on the company?" and "Who else is doing this in my industry?" then you are not calling on an early adopter. Understand that none of these questions are inherently bad, or inappropriate, but they are the types of questions that come from someone who is risk averse. These are prospects that want to take a safe approach. The decisions they make tend to be the safest decisions, not necessarily the most pioneering. However, when prospects ask questions like, "How does it work?" "Why is it good for me?" and "How does it compare to what I'm doing today?" then you are talking to people who are evaluating the merits of the solution that you are offering. These are the pioneering type of prospects. These will be you first customers.

As your company develops, the spectrum of clients that you will seek becomes much wider. You can then include those risk-averse customers as well, because you have all the solid answers for their questions. A common mistake most emerging companies have is that they do not do the right filtering up front to spend their marketing and sales resources on the very focused set of customers who are most likely to buy their new emerging product or service. They call on everyone. If a prospect is willing to accept an appointment, they wrongfully think that they will call on them. There is a very real opportunity cost in spending sales time selling to a prospect that will not buy, even if they are willing to set an appointment. Everyone can be called on as your company matures, but in the first phase, you have to find early adopters.

Naturally, the precursor to all of this is that you have to staff your own organization first, and the exact same thinking must come into play as you hire. You have to find early adopters. While it may be too simplistic to over-categorize, when someone comes to work for a company, they can fall into one of four kinds of categories. The first are people who just basically exist. They work every day somewhere and they don't necessarily have a plan. They don't have focused goals and don't take the time to understand what they like to do for work. As a result, these people are not high achievers and ultimately become cynical. They create sayings like "It's not what you know; it's who you know" and "The rich get richer; the poor get poorer." They tend to be very negative people. There is no sense in taking on this crew. They will find pessimism at every turn, and an emerging business cannot afford to hire these workers.

The next group of people is the wait and see type. They understand what they like to do for work and they want to achieve. However, they hold out on anything that appears to have an element of risk until it is proven to be safe. I think everybody has an uncle or an aunt or some older family member who says late in life, "You know, in 1960 I could have bought the McDonald's franchise for $25,000." Or if you are in the car with them and driving down the street, they may remark, "See that property over there? Ten years ago it could have been purchased for next to nothing, now there is a shopping center there." Their wait and see method of risk avoidance often leads to regret. These type of people are not good employees for an emerging business either, because when one joins a start-up company, there is some inherent risk that this new venture isn't going to work. Although these people are well intentioned, this is too risky of an avenue for them. Make no mistake, these people can be excellent employees, but they are right for the company maybe in year five, when the company is stable and has $100 million of revenue and lots of profits.

The third type of people are those who like to take chances. They see what they want to do. They have a vision for their careers or what they want to achieve, not just personally but professionally. They interview well and they join the company, but the one flaw they have is that they tend to quit when the going gets tough. Each time they join a company it seems like a great idea, but, alas, the challenge is a little harder than they expect, and then they quit in order to join another company that sounds exciting and new. There seems to always be some excuse as to why they didn't succeed, or how the company or their manager caused them to fail. These people are the most dangerous because everything in a start-up is harder than you think and takes longer than you think.

Finally, there are the people who take the time to understand what the business is trying to accomplish. These people know what they like to do for work and can assess if the company is right for them. They are willing to take some calculated risks. When they take a step forward on a venture, they will stick to it. They are relentless. They will throw themselves at a problem. They want to win. They put in an all out effort every single day. If you attract these people early, then you are going to win. Just as you have to select your early adopter clients, you have to find early adopting employees the first day.

The likely source of great employees at the start of a business – at least this is how we did it – is to hire people you have worked with in other organizations throughout your career. You know them and they know you. There is a relationship already there with a certain amount of trust and confidence, and together you take the step to build the company. In our particular case we decided to become a meaningful company quickly, and the first day we had operations running in 17 cities. It wasn't the "out of the garage" type of start-up. Our company was well capitalized, and we went quickly into the marketplace. We did that because the strategy for what we were trying to accomplish required us to reach a reasonable size quickly, so we had to take the step.

One of the things that I found most valuable and that I would recommend to almost anybody starting a business is that you must have a competent

START-UP FUNDAMENTALS

board of directors. Often, a mistake an early entrepreneur might make is to say, "Hey, I have a little company. I didn't raise tens of millions of dollars to start it. What do I need a board of directors for? That is a big-company thing." That is a mistake for any company that plans to be a high-growth business. If you plan on opening up a corner store, and the plan for the rest of your life is to operate the local corner store, then you don't need a board. But if you are trying to launch a business that has aspirations of becoming meaningful and playing a role in the American economy, then you do need a board of directors. That board of directors should include people who have experience that you don't have. And I do mean experience, not just money. You want to have people who possess unique competencies different from each other, and different from you. This board may include a legal or regulatory expert or a political type, but it must include people who have been CEOs or chairmen of other companies. A core competency of any CEO is the ability to attract and retain a high caliber board of directors who have already been down the road you are about to take.

The term "networking" is often used when the subject of a board of directors is discussed. It is true that the CEO and the board of directors have relationships or "networks" across many industries and the value of the company's network is immeasurable. The key question is "How do you use it"?" The absolute wrong thing to do is to call on your network relationships as prospects. Your network should be used to form alliances with other strategic companies that can help you sell your product or service to others. No one likes to get called on by a friend to buy something. I don't like it, and I certainly don't do it. However, if you need to establish a new banking relationship, then you use your board and other networks to get the proper introduction to the financial community that you need, whether it is a senior lender, a mezzanine debt provider, or connections to the equity markets or private-side money. You use those network relationships to advance your company but not as customers. All too often, the term networking is used as a source of new

173

clients. That is a very inefficient use of your network. The relationships you build networking at high levels provide much more value from the introductions and associations they provide your company. In the end, the company's customers must come from its product and solution, its marketing strategy, its sales channel, and the normal course of business. When you are growing your business by using your sales channel and your marketing channel as your means to get customers, you have done it right. Networking is there to create alliances.

Creating the Business Plan and Assessing Risks

I recommend that everybody write a detailed business plan. This process exposes a couple of things. It gives you a chance to exercise the model in all areas. It also becomes the tool that you will use for raising capital. Later, it becomes the tool against which you measure your success. In fact, a well thought-out business plan may uncover risk variables that were not contemplated at first, and, in the end, prevent you from attempting something that has a high degree of failure. I have heard young entrepreneurs remark, "I don't want to take the time to write a business plan. We'll make it up as we go because there are so many other variables that are going to come in to plan. There is no sense in making a detailed business plan. Let's just make an executive summary of the business that we want to get into." That is a mistake. A detailed business plan should also include measurement metrics. How do you know after a year if you are succeeding? You may learn after a year that your business plan may need to be altered. Okay, fine, you alter it. But the plan needs to be established. It gives an opportunity for not just you, but your equity partners or investors, bankers, and, specifically, senior hirers to understand your success plan. Sometimes the business plan can be co-authored by a group of people. But, however it is done, it is required and a lot of thought has to go into it.

When a business is started, there will be a high degree of risk. It tends to be a high-risk, high-reward environment from the beginning. That said, the risk not worth taking is the "knock out" blow. With an emerging business, you are going to take some calculated risks and take some chances. It needs to be done and that is fine. But you never want to put yourself in the situation where the decision that you just made or the risk that you just took, if it doesn't go the way that you expected it to go, wipes out the company. If you just avoid the knockout punch, risk is a normal, manageable thing. You tend to get used to it. I often say that successful entrepreneurs are people who learn how to be comfortable being uncomfortable. If you are able to be comfortable operating with some level of uncertainty, then the challenge is reduced. To assess risk, calculate the downside of what could happen compared to the benefits if it goes the right way. But, once the decision is made, you have to take the step all the way. The worst environments are when someone tries to put one foot in the boat and keep one foot on the dock. You are not going to succeed there. You have to be in the boat or on the dock, and that's true on every issue.

One of the easiest ways of reducing your risk is by choosing clarity ahead of accuracy at all times. You don't have to be right at all times; you just have to be clear at all times so that there is no ambiguity. There are enough challenges in the early stages of an emerging business. There is no sense in introducing ambiguity as another challenge, where people ask, "Which way are we going?" or "How are we on this issue?" There must be clear, concise directions. You take input from people, but you have to be very clear. Clarity will win over accuracy every time.

The Role of the CEO

Whether it is desirable or not, the CEO spends a great deal of the time in the capital area. In business, the lifeblood is cash. If you don't have enough of it, the business may be forced to make decisions that are affordable but not necessarily optimal, which in turn increases the risk in the venture. You have to consider future capital needs before they occur. Raising equity or debt under desperate conditions causes poor decisions and distracts senior management from executing the business plan. While assistance from your board of directors can aid in the process, capital formation is another core competency at the CEO level. Once the capital structure is in place, the CEO role takes a different turn.

There are many successful ways to start and grow a company, but I personally am not in favor of the CEO who, in the beginning, sells the product or service, handles the financial books of the company, does the windows, and, in effect, executes the business as an affordable alternative to hiring a core management team with expertise in each area. These oftentimes tend to be companies that have growth limitations because the hands-on, controlling, entrepreneur style CEO really does like doing the job rather than driving the company. Yes, a CEO needs to have his or her handprint on the business and be very clear with direction and strategy, but I believe short-term and long-term success is more likely with strong management day one. It is expensive, but again, if you have the right market plan, and you have decided whether you are pursuing the "make," "take," or "change" market strategy, you've identified how much capital will be required; you've written a well thought-out business plan; you see the market that you want; you've identified the type of employees you need to have; and you have recruited, trained, and retained those employees. A strong management team will provide the time to think and act on the types of driving issues that the CEO needs to focus on.

The following example best illustrates the role of management. Let's say that one day a memo is issued that declares, "All management, do not report to work," what would happen? The view I agree with is that all the workforce would pretty much do what they did the day before. Orders would be processed. Accounting reports would be produced. Sales would occur. Some would start to question why the company has all these managers in the first place. In fact, things would run without a problem for some period of time. That is, until something changes. It could be an external change in market or competitive forces. It could be internal changes forced by suppliers. It could be a change in the financial community. Once you introduce any type of change, then someone has to decide what is to be done about it. The leader's role is to constantly and quickly manage change to the benefit of the shareholders, employees, and clients of the company.

To understand the rate of change, I like to think of it this way: Let's say we review the decade from 1950 to 1960 and consider what changed during those ten years. One would find that there were changes, to be sure, but compare that decade to the decade from 1980 to 1990. In those ten years we saw the PC land on every desk. We witnessed an entire software industry enhance virtually every business process. Now consider the decade from 1990 to 2000. During those ten years, the Internet connected the world. The financial markets hit an all time high and a devastating decline. The point here is that the rate of change is growing exponentially. Change is happening faster than it ever has before. Since management's critical role is to deal with change, the performance and responsibility of management is becoming increasingly important, not less important. Therefore, the CEO must be comfortable in an environment that changes constantly. Simply put, If you attempt to operate the same way that you have always operated, you're gone. It was not always this way. There was a time in American business when acceptable thinking was, "This is the way we have always done it and that's the way we will continue to do it." Consider the American car industry. Throughout the '70s, the product coming out of Detroit was primarily the same and consistent with the thinking that the consumer will take what we provide them. The success of foreign competition, much more in tune with consumer demands, resulted in market share losses in Detroit. Consider how fast the car industry reacts to consumer demands today. When consumers showed their desire for SUVs, as an example, every automaker had one in the showroom within two years. Today, it is change or die and the key role of the CEO is to make sure that the organization adapts well to the new opportunities that are presented, both internally and externally.

Management Styles

I happen to like to watch the shows on TV that enable you to actually see what goes on in the trauma center of a hospital. Here's an environment when there are, say, ten people in the trauma center and all ten people are extraordinarily bright. They are all educated and experts in their field. They have all proven that they can handle a very taxing intellectual job, and they can work under stress. They are doers. Suddenly, an ambulance delivers a patient who is critically injured from some type of an accident. At that exact moment, all of these smart, well-trained, expert professionals defer 100 percent of the decisions to one individual who starts barking orders. This person is the chief trauma specialist and when he or she gives an order, everyone acts immediately. In effect, all of these bright experienced professionals are working amidst a management style that is nothing short of dictatorship. If, on the other hand, the chief trauma specialist called for 200cc's of some medication and the other workers replied, "Well, 200cc's may be effective, but I found that 150cc's have worked in other cases. In fact, I think there is evidence that supports the use of an entirely different medication. I believe we should reconvene tomorrow after we have reviewed this case in committee and can support a collective recommendation." Clearly, if this path of collaborative, input-driven, committee-style management is used, the patient would die. In this case, committee style democracy kills. The only management style that could work in that type of environment is dictatorship.

That management style would be equally ridiculous if the hospital was deciding what new x-ray system they should purchase. If a manager just came running into the room and said, "We will buy this brand!" and ran out, that would be inappropriate because that is a decision that is made best through extensive research and collaboration. I firmly believe that management styles need to be deployed from the spectrum of collective, total committee input situations all the way to, and including, dictatorship. In other words, if a leader can be characterized by their management style, limitations exist on that person's effectiveness.

If you choose to start a business with high growth intentions and plan on serving as CEO of this new organization, you have chosen to be the leader. Therefore, you had better get used to going forward alone. If you are traveling down a path and have someone at your right and your left, you are part of a group, not leading the group. To lead, you must be in front. That's the whole idea. You must be comfortable with the fact that you will be taking on some decisions, missions, actions, and responsibilities that are yours and yours alone, and some of those decisions may have adverse effects on some individuals. Someone has to do it, and it is not right for every person.. That is not a knock on anybody or a criticism of any kind. They are not a lesser person than someone who does like that kind of work, but it is a type of work and it is not for everyone.

When you are looking to hire entrepreneurial people and key managers in your organization, it is best to ask, "Would I follow this person?" "Is this somebody whose team I want to be on?" "Would I be comfortable with this person at the wheel when something goes wrong?" Because things will go wrong and there is no avoiding it. However, a strong leader will provide clarity and direction, which, in turn, starts the action moving towards a resolution.

Fundamentals

To succeed as a start-up, you have to decide which doorway you are going to use to enter the marketplace: Make, Take, or Change. From there, the next step is to understand what the ultimate goal is. What is the intention of this organization? To be a successful corner grocer or to be the nation's largest grocer? That goal will influence your decisions about your start-up size, capital, and board formation.

You get customers by finding early adopters who are sold through the market channels and sales process that you have decided will be the methods to grow the business. You gain customers solely through your normal sales channel. In this way you know if your solution is truly valuable to the marketplace. You don't get your customers by selling to your network. Rather, you use your network to access relationships that will help you sell to your market.

Finally, management's key role is to manage change. By deploying a full spectrum of management styles from committee collaboration all the way to dictatorship, you use clarity ahead of all else to insure that the organization adapts well to the opportunities and threats presented by the rapidly changing business environment.

Mr. Martucci founded UAC in 1997 and currently serves as the Company's Chairman and CEO. Before founding UAC, Martucci was vice president of sales for GE Capital-ResCom from May 1995 to January 1997. While there, he was responsible for all sales channels, including direct sales, contract sales, distribution and national accounts. Operating with a base of more than $100 million in venture capital, Martucci and his North American-based sales force succeeded in securing contracts supplying local and long-distance telephone service,

START-UP FUNDAMENTALS

cable television and interactive Internet services to 1.2 million apartment units nationwide.

Prior to his work with GE Capital, Martucci worked for RealCom Office Communications, an MFS Communications Company, as vice president/general manager for RealCom's Eastern division. Martucci led the division through the highest growth period in the company's history. Earlier in his career, Martucci served as region manager for Centigram Communications, a San Jose-based manufacturer of voice-processing technology, and was a manufacturer's representative for Richardson, Texas-based VMX (now a part of Avaya, Inc.), which invented and patented voice-store-and-forward technology, commonly known as voice mail.

Martucci serves as chairman of UAC's board of directors. He is also a director on the boards of Interactive Securities, Phoenix Theatre Group, LLC and Woodmont Capital Group, LLC.

Traveling the Road to Reality

Brent R. Tilson
Tilson HR, Inc.
President & CEO

The Most Important Things to Focus on in Starting a Business

The entrepreneur must have a clear vision for their business. Closely linked to vision is creativity. These two must be present for any business venture to have a chance of success. When I started my current business I can remember the day and the moment of the "ah ha". Over the next few months the idea continued to germinate and the ideas continued to expand. I used my CPA and business consulting experience to analyze the idea and try to shoot holes in it. The critical things I looked at were:

Market capacity
Current lifecycle of the industry
Growth
Declining
Stagnant
Cash flow & Capital Requirements

Each of these areas is critical in assessing whether a business idea has legs. Over the years, many individuals have come to me to help them write business plans or to discuss a business idea and I always use these criteria to explore the opportunity. Often these business ideas failed to meet my basic requirements.

Market Capacity

During my time as a practicing CPA, I worked with many different businesses from large to small businesses. What I realized was that the businesses that were successful had large market capacity – whether it was a very specific niche or a general market, what enabled them to grow was market capacity. Thus, a first litmus test for a new business is to determine if the market has enough capacity for more players. So for me, the thing is to make sure that when you start a business there is opportunity for growth and opportunity for success. If a market is declining or dying, that is not the business to get into.

Industry Lifecycle

Each business and product offering has a lifecycle of birth, growth, and decline. In order to jump-start a business it is critical to understand where the business offerings are in the industry lifecycle. If a business offering is during the birth stage of an industry, costs to get the product to market and acceptance is traditionally significant compared to entering the market after the early movers have spent their money and made their mistakes. The ideal time to enter into a market is during the early stages of the growth cycle. During this time, costs are not as significant and customers are becoming aware of the product/service offerings on a broader scale. Entering a market in the stagnant or declining lifecycle is a recipe for failure. Very few companies can overcome declining market trends to become successful unless they are providing a new disruptive technology or service, which would cause the industry to move back to the growth stage.

Cash Flow

The ultimate goal of any business is to convert resources into products and services that will generate positive cash flow and ultimately profits. The speed at which the resources can be turned into cash is extremely critical. The longer this cycle, the more capital is required to fund the business as companies must invest in product development, inventory, and overhead. The entrepreneur needs to calculate their cash flow cycle and determine the burn rate of cash until sales climb high enough to generate a positive cash flow. Thus, to jump-start a successful company, an entrepreneur must balance the expenditure of cash with the cash flow lifecycle to get a company to cash flow positive as quickly as possible. Otherwise additional capital will be required and may be difficult to attract if the entrepreneur did not meet their original plan or miscalculated the business model. The next important step is to develop a solid financial model. Can this new business actually provide goods or services that are faster, better, and cheaper than those currently available? Alternatively, if this is a displacement product or service, will it pull market spend or share from the products it is targeted to replace? If it is a new product or service, what is the price point to get those early adopters to write the check? Many businesses fail due to a less than thought through financial model. In my case, I developed my initial pricing model based upon market research and other modeling tools. During the early years my financial model stayed relatively stable, however, I continued to tinker with price points and service offerings.

Once the market capacity and financial modeling are developed, the entrepreneur must focus on developing the rest of a solid business plan. There are many off the shelf software products that can greatly assist in the development of the business plan. After the plan is written, it is time to test the idea. Take the plan and give it to business owners and advisors for their input.

One point that served to be very important in growing my business was to focus on one service and do it very well. I did not want to try to offer more services than I could support. I believe that as a company grows, additional products and services can be successfully provided and supported, however, in the early life of a business a very focused service or product is critical. I like to think of a business much like a Christmas tree. Initially, the business is like a small tree and there are only so many ornaments (products/services) that can be hung on the tree without it looking cluttered and ugly. As the tree grows, more ornaments can be added and ultimately the size of the tree supports many types of ornaments, all of which complement the overall look of the tree. I have seen many businesses who have added to many products and services too early in their lives and the business never grows and, ultimately, is unsuccessful.

I have seen many good business plans and great ideas never develop into successful profitable businesses. I believe one of the reasons is that the entrepreneur does not understand the lifecycle that every business will go through. I actually have a diagram that I show to people. It's on an XY axis, with a wavy line going up the middle – like an "S". I've been using this for years to explain that a business has three phases. There is the start-up phase, then the growth phase, and then the realignment phase. And what's important is that people understand that there are very specific things that they need to focus on during each of those phases. If they understand that going into it, then it will help them better manage the business.

When you're starting the business, you're in phase one – you're in start-up. This phase is all about sales and controlling spending. I think it's very important to be mindful of where you spend your money. I'm very careful to manage my expenses compared to revenue; in order for me to spend money, I have to have a revenue result from it. And if not, I'm going to be very, very careful to spend that discretionary money. You don't want to put yourself in a position where your overhead will eat you up.

As already mentioned, it's also important to make sure that the business you're starting actually has market capacity. If it doesn't, don't do it. Don't go into a business that you can't possibly grow exponentially. Otherwise, you're going to have a small retail store in some small strip mall, and you'll make $40,000 a year at best, and you'll have to work your tail off. How many businesses do you drive by and say, "There's no way that that company can possibly make enough money to pay anybody?" I see it everyday. I'll walk into a store and wonder, "Why did you start this business? There's no way you can make money here." And I'll see businesses that join us as clients and we become their employer, and I see that they've been around for years, but the person who owns it only pays himself $45,000 a year but he has all the risk and all the responsibility – he just doesn't have any market capacity. It's the wrong business. It was a poor choice. But he's in it and he can't get out of it.

I see a lot of companies that tend to be very inwardly focused and don't put as much emphasis in the sales side as they should. Or the CEO is a technician and he started this new company because he knows a lot about the product, but he's not a salesperson. The CEO is the best salesperson – he has to be if the company is going to be successful out of the gate; if not, they need to get somebody who believes in it just as much. But I think too many people stay in the office. They don't go out and grow their business like they need to. Sales is from 8:00 to 5:00; working in the office is after 5:00. And I think that's the problem in a lot of companies – it's where they allocate and spend their time. They need to systemize and get things in place internally; things have to be very simple in the early stages of a start-up company so they can focus on sales. Obviously product has to be there – I'm assuming there's a product – but the sales are critical. You can come up with the best idea, but if people don't buy, then it's only an idea. I think the real "aha" moment for every company should be when sales are coming in – people are acknowledging that this is a good service or product, and they're buying it.

So I think it's very important in the start-up phase to understand how to keep costs down, understand the capacity, and understand that sales are critical. And then after that people have to realize that they have to quickly move from that entrepreneurial stage and that sales stage, and they need to start backfilling so that they can get into the growth stage. Because if they are never able to leverage other people within their business – by adding quality people and putting them into very specific areas – they will never achieve the next phase, which is growth. They'll always stay in that first phase, the start-up, because they can never get beyond it. Ultimately growth will slow and companies enter into a critical phase. Either realign and continue growing or possibly die. I like to call this the realignment stage. During this stage, companies must look closely at market trends, the business they are in, displacement technologies that may force them out of business or have a significant negative impact on sales, and make the necessary changes to their business models to survive and thrive. So they need to understand each of those phases and understand what they need to do in each one to get to the next stage in the life cycle.

The Role of Networking

Networking was very important for me in starting my business. At the time I started my company, I didn't know that there was actually what is known as the professional employer organization industry. All I knew was that many of my accounting clients had needs, and I thought I'd found an effective way to perhaps solve those problems. Then when I started researching, I realized that there, in fact, was an industry already doing some of the things that I was thinking about doing. It was interesting to come across the concept of what I wanted to do, and then to find out that some other people were doing it as well.

When I first started my company, I just modeled some of the pricing models off of industry information I was able to find – it was hard to find, but I did find some. But when I first started getting out in the market and growing and networking, it was a very new concept. Most people had never heard of the idea of letting someone become the employer for another company's work force – not like a temporary agency, but truly becoming the employer. (I go into a company and say, "Let me become the employer of all these people, and I will manage all

189

the details of employment, and, essentially, you're outsourcing to me all the employment responsibilities and headaches.") That concept was a very difficult sale back in 1995 because, especially here in the Midwest, things tend to migrate slowly and the concept of outsourcing – not just payroll but outsourcing and letting someone else be the employer – was very difficult. So networking was very important for me but, to be honest, at that time, I didn't truly appreciate the power of networking within a marketplace. I went out and called on people – and I have a fairly successful small accounting firm and I know a lot of people – but I didn't truly understand the concept of creating really strong relationships through networking.

And then, around 1996, I read one of Peter Drucker's books, *The Executive Handbook*, which talks about how not all products are homogeneous or not all markets are homogeneous. And I realized that I was treating my product as a homogeneous product, trying to sell the same service to all companies. But there truly is a difference between a five-employee company and a hundred-employee company, and the needs that they have are truly different. I was trying to sell the same package of services to everyone, and I was getting different push backs from the different groups. One group would say, "I don't need all these things; all I want is this." The other group would say, "I need more than just that; I want all these things." And so I found that I needed to retool my product because I was only selling it at one level.

At the same time, I read another article about innovative product adoption, which argued that innovative products are not purchased because they are innovative and make people better; people typically adopt new innovative products because they know someone else who's using that product. And I thought, "That's what I need to address."

I had two basic issues in my company. One was the fact that I needed to change my product from being a homogeneous product to something that was tailored and scalable, but I also needed to find a different way of marketing because early on I was struggling to get people to buy into the concept.

So I started aggressively pursuing networking. I thought of who would be the most innovative adopters within my marketplace, and I looked at a number of publications to find out who the thought leaders were and which companies said in their marketing materials that they were entrepreneurial and thought leaders, and I marketed to those firms. Since that time, we have become one of the most plugged-in companies within this marketplace. Our clients are the top law firms, the top venture capital firms. We have really leveraged networking at a very high level, and what we found was that, in our marketplace, by getting in with a certain group of companies that were considered the thought leaders, people now put us in that same area. So when a deal happens, often we're involved and engaged in the opportunity as the company is being formed – they bring us in at the beginning, and it's because we're a part of that networked group.

If I were advising someone on starting an effective network, I would say first to develop a matrix identifying those types of people who would do business with them. So, for example, let's say they're an IT consulting firm and they want to sell to professional service firms. I would recommend that they ask who would be the companies that most likely would use their services. If it's law firms – we know law firms are heavy users of computer technology – then find out who would refer them into law firms. How can they get involved? Maybe it's the bar association, or maybe it's other vendors that sell to law firms. They should try to develop a matrix of types of referring sources, and then break that down into major groups and decide within each group what value that group would gain from the relationship. Networking can't be one-sided; it needs to lead to relationships in which both parties can value the knowledge or opportunities shared.

Vision and Goals

Writing a business plan is extremely important. A business plan gives you the opportunity as an entrepreneur to lay out your vision. Without that vision, it's very difficult to know if you're being successful, to know what direction you're going everyday, to be able to make decisions. Many people write a business plan, and then it just sits on the shelf and they never look at it again, but I believe it's a living, breathing document that has to be amended continually.

I'm an eternal optimist, so sometimes my goals tend to be a little aggressive, and my board of directors has to dial me in at times because I tend to really try to push the envelope on the goals we have for the business. I think setting goals is a discipline that people learn as time goes on because many times when I look at companies, especially when they're first starting up, they tend to have unrealistic goals. In the first few years of any business, it's very difficult. You can guess and say, "This is what I think we're going to sell," or "This is the goal we have for volume, and this is the goal for profit," but until there's actually some history behind the company, it's difficult to really give good measurements – or good guesses, as that's really all you're doing.

In setting our goals, we look at a number of different factors. We look at history, we look at trends, we look at market capacity, and then we also look at what we believe we as a company can accomplish. That's how we establish goals – we say, "Based on this information that we have, we should be able to have this much in sales this next year. We should be able to grow by this amount."

It's very difficult in a company that's growing fast to really have a good indication of where the company is at any given time. It's like driving a car with a mud covered windshield and mud down the sides, only a couple of indicators on the dash are working, and you're driving 150 miles an hour. Often that's what the CEO's job feels like because you think you can see the future, but often all you're basing it on is information that's historical. It's very difficult to know how to drive the car when things are not clear.

So we've taken on the idea of creating dashboards, or bulletin boards, in each area of the company – sales, accounting, operations, and so on – with critical indicators of how the business is performing. So, for example, in sales they have the key sales charts and graphs and targets and pipeline reports all posted, so I can walk down the hall and look on their bulletin board and see a snapshot – basically, the gauges, if you will – of what the sales department is doing. It's updated every few weeks. I wish it could be done daily – I wish it could be on my computer, but it's not there yet – but it's one of those things that allow me to help those areas set goals and keep the progress visible. It's not in somebody's notepad; it's not in somebody's mind; it's up on the board.

So when it comes to setting goals, it's a matter of looking at the company and identifying the targets that we want to hit. More important, though, is measuring the results and making sure that we're actually making progress – so we can respond if we're not. The dashboard concept is helpful because it enables everybody to see, and you can bring it down to the level that's necessary for people to understand what's important for their areas to accomplish.

Assessing Risk

I analyze risk in many ways. There is economic risk, property risk, financial risk, outside risk, and employment risk. All the different areas of a business constitute a level of risk, but risk is something that people don't pay enough attention to.

INSIDE THE MINDS

You can insure certain risks. For me, it's really looking at each of the areas of our company and trying to evaluate what risks exist, and then trying to figure out, "Is it a risk I just want to ignore?" There may be some risks you just can't do anything about. The risk of war, for example, is not something you can control. But it would have an impact on some businesses. So for my company, I try to ask, "What can I control? What can't I control? And then how do I go about managing that risk the best I can?"

One example of risk is financial risk of our clients. Do they have the ability to pay? That has been a real risk over the last year and a half. We had to take a very aggressive approach to late payments, where before we might not have been as concerned. Now we don't have any tolerance for slow pay because we know the risk that a company could have – that things could be going badly for that company. We terminated a few companies last year that we might have tried to work with before – and a couple of those companies actually went out of business, so those turned out to be good decisions. So there are many different risks, but we try to identify and put them in categories and then decide how to go about managing those risks.

Management Style

In terms of my management style, I would say I try to lead by example, but I try to act more like a coach. If we were a sports team, I'd try to put the people in the positions they need to be in, I'd try to give them the knowledge they need, and then I'd try to make sure that everybody's doing what needs to be done to make the team as successful as it can be. It's not an autocratic style at all; in fact, it's more of a development style: Here are the areas we need to focus on, these are your responsibilities, these are your goals. That's why we're putting the dashboards in each of the areas, so people can help better manage themselves. They can see

194

TRAVELING THE ROAD TO REALITY

where things are and what they need to focus on. I see myself as trying to develop people to be more responsible for themselves and their areas, and my role as being a support person and a visionary leader for the company.

I've been thinking a lot about how company leaders have to change their style and the information they share with their company as it grows. When the company was small, and there were only a few people here, people knew the vision because we worked together every day. Now, while I may be in the office, the things that I'm working on tend to be different than what the rest of the staff is working on. I've learned as time has gone on – and especially growing as fast as we have – that in order to keep people motivated, I have to find ways to bring people together and talk about the things that are exciting, the things we're doing, and the areas we need to work on. I try to find ways to share good information, and I also try to be critical when things aren't going the way I want them to. And I'm really the cheerleader for where I want things to go in the future.

Brent R. Tilson is the Chairman, CEO, and President of Tilson HR which Mr. Tilson co-founded in 1995. Mr. Tilson has orchestrated the growth and success of Tilson HR from a start-up in 1995 to being ranked one of the fastest growing private companies in the nation. Inc magazine recognized Tilson HR as #11 in 2001 followed by #48 in the 2002 Inc 500 List. In addition, Tilson HR was named the fastest growing privately owned business in Indianapolis in 2000, according to the Indianapolis Business Journal. The Johnson Center for Entrepreneurship & Innovation at Indiana University has awarded Tilson HR the Indiana Growth 100 award for four consecutive years. Under his direction, the Company has achieved a cumulative annual growth rate over the past 5 years of 3,092%. Human Resources Outsourcing Today (HRO Today) listed Tilson HR as one of the recommended Professional Employer

195

Organizations (PEOs) & Administrative Service Organizations (ASOs) in its October 2002 issue.

Mr. Tilson, a 2000, 2001, and 2002 Ernst & Young Entrepreneur of the Year® finalist, is very active in the Indianapolis business community and is a member of the 2000 class of "40 Under 40," an award given each year by the Indianapolis Business Journal recognizing Indiana's top young executives. He was selected as one of the leading executives in the PEO industry in 1999. In 1997, he successfully negotiated a stock and strategic alliance relationship with Personnel Management, Inc. (formerly TPMI:NASDAQ), one of Indiana's largest temporary staffing companies. Mr. Tilson also successfully negotiated an important federal policy relating to minority business contracts with the Small Business Administration, greatly strengthening the PEO industry.

A CPA, Mr. Tilson graduated from Indiana University School of Business and started his working career with KPMG Peat Marwick. Mr. Tilson started his own accounting practice in 1992 specializing in small to medium sized businesses, which he sold in 1998. His background as a CPA includes: business development, corporate and international taxation, state and local taxation, benefits and compensation, mergers and acquisitions, and finance and restructuring.

Mr. Tilson is in frequent demand to speak to industries, associations, and other organizations about strategic business planning, human resource solutions, and business process outsourcing.

Adapting to Your Customer

David Paul Taylor
TeleSynthesis, Inc.
President

TeleSynthesis

TeleSynthesis was founded in 1997 to provide software engineering services to the telecommunications industry. TeleSynthesis, a true bootstrap start-up, was launched with seed funding provided by the co-founders and a small SBA loan.

TeleSynthesis was launched to pursue the development and deployment of software that allowed telecommunications service providers to exchange customer information in support of a federal mandate. Our idea was ahead of its time so we pursued contract software engineering work to survive. TeleSynthesis, with in-depth telecom domain expertise and advanced object oriented design and programming skills, was well prepared to perform the heavy lifting required by high tech companies such as Lucent Technologies and Tekelec. During 1998 and 1999, we sold specifically to the telecom industry. This changed late in 1999 when our largest customer, a telecom equipment vendor, advised us that they would not spend any money on contract software engineering services in the year 2000. The impending telecom meltdown was already affecting TeleSynthesis.

In response to the equipment vendor's news, TeleSynthesis diversified the business into other industry verticals such as healthcare, travel, entertainment, and finance. As a result of the diversification, TeleSynthesis achieved a ranking of twenty-fifth on the Inc 500 list of fastest growing private companies. The key to our success was our ability to diversify the business. This chapter examines how TeleSynthesis evolved to enable diversification.

The Idea

Every business starts with an idea. When TeleSynthesis was founded, our original idea was to provide telecom service providers with a software system required by the Telecommunications Act of 1996. The Telecom Act of '96 mandated local number portability a business environment that allowed customers to keep their telephone number when they changed service providers. As a result, telecom service providers were required to exchange customer information with other telecom service providers when a customer changed from one service provider to another. In essence, the Telecom Act of '96 required competitors to cooperate for the benefit of the customer.

This unprecedented ruling required an unprecedented system and TeleSynthesis set out to build it. Unfortunately, the capabilities and systems we envisioned would not be deployed for several years. TeleSynthesis, being a true bootstrap company, lacked the funding necessary to wait out the market. We abandoned our original idea of building the unprecedented system and pursued survival strategies.

Our survival strategy was to market our software development capabilities on a contract basis to the telecommunications industry. We reasoned that our combination of telecommunications expertise and software engineering skills was rare and of value to the telecom industry. The survival strategy carried the company for the next two years as the Internet and telecommunications industries exploded. Within two years, the Internet and telecommunication industry slowdown was upon us. TeleSynthesis found that we could no longer count on the combination of telecommunications expertise and software engineering skills for survival. TeleSynthesis observed that industry verticals such as finance, entertainment, energy, and travel were not struggling quite as much as the telecommunications industry. We reasoned that we could develop software for other industries without in-depth domain expertise if we learned how to leverage our customers' understanding of their business. After minor adjustments to our software development methodology, TeleSynthesis began to partner with our customers in various industries. Our ability to define and nurture these symbiotic relationships on a customer-by-customer basis was the key to our survival, and the key to the growth that earned TeleSynthesis a ranking of twenty-fifth on the Inc500's list of fastest growing private companies.

New businesses are created based on ideas. Some ideas work and some don't. As we learned at TeleSynthesis, an idea alone doesn't ensure success. Success requires the ability to recognize a good idea coupled with the ability to transform the idea into reality.

On the Road to Reality

Being blessed, some say cursed, with a brilliant idea is the starting point of a long journey in which you will transport your idea from concept to reality. The transportation analogy is useful because your idea can be considered to be the cargo in a delivery vehicle. It is important to fully understand the distinction between the cargo and the vehicle because they represent two different types of people. The person who sketched the original idea, the cargo, on the back of the napkin is an *inventor*. The person who designs and builds the vehicle used to transport the cargo is an *entrepreneur*. Then, of course, you need someone to drive the vehicle. The driver is the CEO or COO. When you are interested in fast-tracking a company, you must understand the responsibilities, contribution, and personality traits of each of these individuals.

In the case of TeleSynthesis, the cargo was software engineering services and the company was the vehicle for the delivery of the cargo. The entrepreneurs were co-founders David Taylor and David Mendes. The

ADAPTING TO YOUR CUSTOMER

driver today is David Taylor. TeleSynthesis was able to survive and flourish because the vehicle we built was capable of transporting several similar types of cargo.

Many good ideas reach fruition slowly or not at all because the inventor doesn't recognize the requirements of entrepreneurship and mistakenly fulfills the role. The inventor staring at the idea on the back of the napkin faces the first crossroad on the road to reality: deciding whether or not they will fulfill the responsibilities of the entrepreneur. Making a bad decision at this crossroad has a negative affect on the whole journey. To make a sound decision at this crossroad the inventor must assess how their personality traits compare to those of an entrepreneur. The following paragraphs describe the key characteristics of entrepreneurship as they pertain to TeleSynthesis.

Vision

The vision represented by the idea on the back of the napkin is only the impetus for starting the business. Just as there is a vision of the idea, the cargo, there must be a vision for the delivery vehicle, the company. The entrepreneur or the CEO normally establishes the company's initial vision. In addition to the overall company objectives, the entrepreneur must envision aspects of the business such as the corporate values and culture, the organization, the company identity, the type of people required to make the organization function well.

Vision, or unusual foresight, is a combination of intuition and idealism. These two characteristics are not usually found in the engineering profession where the preferred employee characteristics are the ability to analyze and realism. Because TeleSynthesis consisted of a high percentage of people with an engineering bias, we struggled to define a corporate vision initially. We knew we wanted to build a software

201

engineering company that provided maximum return on our customer's software investment, but we couldn't envision how we would do this. Fortunately for TeleSynthesis, the market for our services was hot and we were able to survive by reacting to the market. TeleSynthesis recognized that in order to grow beyond our survival phase, we needed to be less reactionary and more visionary. To accomplish this goal TeleSynthesis created the Chief Strategy Officer position, which was filled by David Taylor. This action put TeleSynthesis in a position to grow out of survival mode and into a mode that allowed TeleSynthesis to exploit market opportunities.

Often strategic business decisions are based on intuition. This is a leap of faith that is difficult for people who need to analyze the facts at hand in order to make a decision. The problem analytical people have in the early stages of a business cycle is at that time most of the facts are unclear or unknown. In such cases, an analytical person who needs facts to make a decision will certainly struggle. An intuitive person, on the other hand, is capable of making an accurate decision based on the limited facts available. Intuition is an interesting gift that is often misunderstood in business where less intuitive people are the norm. Because there is not usually a wealth of information to analyze when it comes to launching a business, an entrepreneur should be somewhat intuitive.

A person who is less intuitive can use idealism to define a company's vision. Idealism is the practice of seeing situations the way they should be and not the way they actually are. Thankfully, even the most hardened realist can envision perfect-world scenarios for transporting an idea to reality if necessary.

Organization and Business Architecture

The inventor is the owner of the idea but the entrepreneur is the architect of the business. A good business architect is a person who has the ability to quickly understand the business requirements and has the ability to design an organization that addresses the requirements. Effective organizational design requires a person who is a high-level, top-down thinker. The architect of an organization is less detail oriented. They tend to think big and not small.

Hierarchical approach to organization

In the case of software development we recognize four high-level functions: 1.) Marketing, 2.) Sales, 3.) Engineering, and 4.) Construction. Each of these four functions has an average three key phases. This means that your organization from end-to-end consists of twelve key phases. If each key phase can be broken down into three key activities your organization consists of thirty-six key activities from end-to-end. If you add one more level of detail by decomposing the activities into three tasks, you have one hundred eight tasks strung together.

The point being detail oriented individuals think of their organizations at this level. They are more comfortable seeing a process map with one hundred eight boxes strung together than just four. We initially faced this situation at TeleSynthesis because detail oriented individuals who did not think in a hierarchical fashion designed our software development process. The result was an unwieldy, poorly understood method of operating that made us inefficient. A hierarchical thinker eventually redesigned the process, fixing the problem.

The real danger with this type of person is their attention to detail compromises their ability to expand and enlarge the company. They become lost in minutia and lose sight of the over-arching requirements of the business. The phrase "They can't see the forest for the trees" accurately describes this situation. The business architect for your company cannot be this type of individual. If the process map for your company consists of a chain of more than four to six interconnected boxes at the highest level, you are likely seeing the trees of your business architecture and not the forest.

Delegation

The entrepreneur as the business architect designs the organization and must empower a team to run the company. In fact, the entrepreneur may delegate all responsibility for running the company to the CEO. Although it is necessary for the entrepreneur to pay close attention to the details of the business when it is small, the entrepreneur cannot micromanage the company or the management team if the business is to grow quickly, or at all. In order for the company to grow successfully, the entrepreneur must have the confidence to delegate authority and responsibility to key individuals. At TeleSynthesis we found that delegation made our detail oriented individuals uncomfortable because they didn't like giving up control of the details. This attitude is appropriate for employees who are responsible for specific tasks, but it is inappropriate for the management team. If members of your management have trouble delegating authority, you will have trouble expanding the company under these individuals. If the entrepreneur has trouble delegating authority, the chances the company will ever be on the fast track are very small. TeleSynthesis eventually removed all the managers who were incapable of delegation.

Another benefit of delegation is the exploitation of specialization. Nobody, no matter how highly they regard their abilities, can perform every function in the company better than certain individuals who have special skills. It is tempting for the entrepreneur who built the business from the ground up to believe they can perform every function better than the next person. This is only true for a short time in the early stages of the business. Once the company begins to generate traction, the entrepreneur must seek specialists for every position and allow them to perform their job without interfering.

To facilitate delegation, TeleSynthesis created a framework for management and employee decisions. We then empowered the management team and employees to make decisions within the framework. Our framework is defined by our corporate values and our corporate culture. Most employees, whether they have management responsibilities or not, appreciate operating within the framework. It provided them with guidelines in which to make their decisions. Being empowered to make their own decisions instilled a sense of ownership in each decision maker. By creating the framework for the company's decision making process, TeleSynthesis provided a tool that helped individuals who felt uncomfortable delegating authority function appropriately.

Confidence and Sound Judgment

The entrepreneur generally develops confidence through their past experiences. Confidence is also gained by knowing that whatever mistakes you might make, you can fix. Confidence is required to sell the vision and the organization to employees, customers, and potential investors.

Confidence allows the entrepreneur to accept risk. The smaller the company, the more personal risk the entrepreneur usually accepts. TeleSynthesis was started using the co-founder's funds. Unlike many technology companies launched with large amounts of venture capital during the Internet craze, TeleSynthesis co-founders had the confidence required to risk their own funds to provide the company's initial working capital.

Persuasiveness

The strength of one's convictions is the foundation for an entrepreneur's persuasiveness. Excellent communication skills, not necessarily charisma, are required to sell investors, employees, and your management team your vision. The grander your vision, the more persuasive you must be. An entrepreneur, especially one without a proven track record, must craft their communication carefully to ensure the audience understands the message. Because TeleSynthesis is a technology company, our communications were often highly technical and sometimes missed the mark with our business customers. This situation was our attempt to overcome our lack of a business track record. The situation was corrected as TeleSynthesis matured as a business.

Leadership

Leadership is the ability to guide, direct and influence. The aforementioned traits contribute to one's ability to lead. An inventor is a person who identifies or recognizes opportunities before other people do. An entrepreneur is a person who is willing to act upon that opportunity – to take the business risks required to capitalize on the opportunity. A successful entrepreneur is someone with the leadership skills necessary to design, build, and empower an organization of specialists who work together to exploit the opportunity.

ADAPTING TO YOUR CUSTOMER

When you are sitting staring at the napkin with your great idea on it, you've arrived at that first crossroad on the road to reality. You must now decide whether you are the inventor, the entrepreneur, or both. It is time for an honest self-assessment of your capabilities. One of the hardest facts you must face is just because it's your idea, doesn't mean you are qualified to be the entrepreneur. This is often made mistake is a result of inventors not understanding the responsibilities of the entrepreneur. These individuals usually have an appetite for being the boss. It's your idea. You started the company. This is your call. When you consider this important decision remember the words of the well-known movie character that said: "A person has to know their limitations." If you are interested in building a solid company fast, this will be your first key decision.

If you can't honestly say that you generally fit the profile described above, the best decision you can make is to hire someone who does. You may start the company and run it for a time, but you must be willing to turn it over to a qualified entrepreneur as soon as is practical. You must also be aware of the trap of the new CEO. This is a situation where an under-qualified person starts a company and becomes enamored with their power. The new CEO then convinces themselves that they are capable of running the company and becomes unwilling to let go. The new CEO may eventually be successful, but their eventual success will come at the expense of efficiency. The company will not likely achieve fast-track momentum because the new CEO will spend too much time learning the job. The new CEO will face many a crossroad. At each crossroad the new CEO faces decisions that can lead to a dead end or to a long circuitous road to reality. Few of the crossroads are well-marked and are hard for the untrained eye to distinguish. It is always more efficient to have someone who has actually driven the road to reality before they attempt to drive your vehicle.

207

The Roadmap

The roadmap used by the entrepreneur to transport the idea to reality is the company's business plan. Typically, new CEOs or inventors use the business plan as a mechanism to secure funding for their company. They create plans focused on their idea but lacking in the definition of the delivery vehicle. Early TeleSynthesis business plans were of this nature. When TeleSynthesis was founded, we fully understood our software engineering process, but we didn't fully understand all the requirements of running a business. Like many start-up companies, we understood our idea but we were only learning how to build the company. Because TeleSynthesis was a true bootstrap start-up, our underdeveloped business plans did not compromise our funding objectives, but they did compromise our ability to expand efficiently. Our initial organization was designed to only support our engineering process. Our engineering process includes the analysis, design, and development functions of software development. As we matured as an organization, we recognized the need for a sales function and a marketing function ahead of the engineering functions. The key learning experiences are now reflected in our business plan that fully describes all aspects of our road to reality.

Your business plan must capture your vision, your business objectives, the method, and organization you'll use to accomplish your objectives. Objectives vary from business to business. TeleSynthesis measures our success based on three criteria. The first criterion is our financial effectiveness. The second is customer satisfaction and the third is employee satisfaction. We map these three corporate objectives into the objectives of each company function. This mapping ensures that the objectives for each function support the corporate objectives.

The entrepreneur leads the initial planning activities. During planning meetings, the entrepreneur must insist upon idealistic goals. Idealism is the practice of seeing situations as they should be versus as they actually

ADAPTING TO YOUR CUSTOMER

are. Idealism is on the opposite end of the spectrum from reality. As the entrepreneur, you should be envisioning a perfect world. Assume you start with a spectrum from zero to one hundred with zero being reality and one hundred being completely idealistic. When you deal with customers, they will always interject a dose of reality into your dealings. We reasoned that halfway was fair for both parties. We learned that customers expected to negotiate with us, and they expected for us to make concessions during our negotiations. If we didn't make concessions, the customer thought we were unreasonable. We found in our business dealings that we were continually meeting the customer halfway. This created a win-win scenario for TeleSynthesis and our customers.

The key to success in customer negotiations and in any planning activities is to define an opening negotiating position that is idealistic. TeleSynthesis, as a conservative engineering firm, would not allow ourselves to think in an idealistic fashion. Instead of the outcome of our planning activities rating one hundred on the idealistic scale, our internal outcome was in a range of fifty to sixty. We found we were being too realistic in setting our goals. What we didn't understand was that we were setting the bar too low for the company. When we established our opening negotiating position at fifty on the idealism scale and dealt with a customer whose open negotiating position was zero, we reached a middle ground of twenty-five. If our opening negotiating position was one hundred, we would reach a middle ground of fifty with the customer. This position is more favorable to TeleSynthesis and it is still perceived as win-win by the customer. The difference between the two approaches in this example is twenty-five (fifty versus twenty-five) points on the idealism scale. This difference represents the difference between mediocrity and success.

The entrepreneur must always establish and defend the idealistic point of view even in the face of stiff disagreement from the realists in the

209

company. If you don't successfully defend the idealistic position, internally your company will face reduced expectations and results due to the cumulative affect of your internal and external compromises. Your company will be mediocre.

We establish idealist objectives internally much to the dismay of some of the management team. The argument they have against setting idealistic objectives is that they are unrealistic and you can never meet idealist goals. If you know you're not going to meet your objectives and you're going to have to settle for reaching more realistic objectives, why set them so high in the first place? The answer, of course, is to make the company reach. We always revisit the idealism topic in our planning sessions. It seems like an annoyance but it is a sure-fire method of getting the management team engaged and working together.

The key objective for the entrepreneur during the planning process is to guide the management team toward the acceptance of the idealistic objectives. Upon completion of the planning process, the management team must understand and sign up to meeting the objectives. Each member of the management team must also have a plan of how their function can meet the objectives.

Once the plan is agreed to and in effect, the entrepreneur can use the business plan to monitor the progress of the company. We review our plan quarterly at a minimum. Reviewing the plan regularly and holding the management team accountable for their objectives establishes the plan as a business tool. Tying the management team's compensation to the business plan objectives ensures the tool will be used effectively.

Initially companies should plan to start out somewhat slowly until they are sure the vehicle they've built is roadworthy. It's also easier to win smaller deals with smaller customers before you are established. It is much easier to access the high-level decision makers in smaller companies. Access to these individuals allows you to create customer intimacy quickly and effectively because you can tailor your service offerings on a case-by-case basis.

To facilitate growth, the plan should focus on marketing. This is difficult for companies that struggle with vision because marketing is the component of the business that explains your vision externally. More importantly, marketing enables sales. Effective marketing is more than hype – it creates an environment in which your sales team can be successful. Once your sales team is successful, sales will drive growth.

The Vehicle

The vehicle that delivers your idea is your organization and infrastructure. There are a number of ways to fund the creation of your vehicle. TeleSynthesis chose to bootstrap the company using just-in-time hiring to build the company. In this approach, our sales organization, our products or services delivery organization, and our human resources organization were trained in a TeleSynthesis-designed just-in-time hiring process in which the organizations were closely linked and in constant communication. Because TeleSynthesis mastered this technique even in a time when technology candidates were expecting BMWs as signing bonuses, we were able to grow efficiently.

Your business, your vehicle, is a team of people who are following the roadmap for the business. A well-designed organization allows the team members to focus on their areas of responsibility. A well-staffed organization is a team consisting of specialists in each area of responsibility. The entrepreneur is the leader of the team who provides overall guidance, but is not involved in the day-to-day activities of any area of the business as a normal course of operations.

To build a management capable of fast-tracking a company, you must hire specialists who have prior experience in their jobs. While this sounds obvious, the opposite occurs in many start-up companies because founders tend to hire people they are comfortable with. In cases where the entrepreneur is a novice, the entrepreneur will be tempted to hire novice managers. It's human nature to want to hire and work with someone like yourself – in this case, inexperienced. This is an ill-advised practice for a number of reasons. The first is managers without the requisite experience must learn their jobs before they can help the company gain and sustain traction. This limits their effectiveness. Also, the entrepreneur runs the risk of hiring a person who may be unable to grow into the job. Their inability to grow into the job only becomes obvious after time has passed, making correcting the problem difficult.

Even more importantly, hiring people you are comfortable with can compromise the diversity of your team. Diversity is the key to a successful management team because each management position has diverse responsibilities and the best candidate for each position will have a distinct personality type. Successful salesman and marketers are more flamboyant and aggressive than accountants and engineers who tend to be quiet and reserved. If the entrepreneur is an engineer who doesn't embrace diversity, they will have problems hiring the best salesman. To fill management positions effectively requires the ability to hire and manage diverse personality types. To achieve the all-important chemistry between diverse personality types, the entrepreneur must create a structure, an organization, and a corporate culture in which diverse personalities can work together in a complementary fashion. Initially, TeleSynthesis did not fully understand the need for diversity in the company and had a tendency to hire people who had the personality traits of engineers for every position. This approach not only compromised specialization of responsibilities, it created an environment where the managers viewed their peers as competitors instead of teammates.

ADAPTING TO YOUR CUSTOMER

Teamwork results from building chemistry between the diverse personality types. A successful entrepreneur will have the ability to create team chemistry. This requires an understanding of human nature and the ability to accurately assess personality types when building the team. When hiring, the entrepreneur must assess the candidate's potential contribution based on their experience and their ability to work as a member of the team. When selecting a management team member, it is fairly easy to identify a team player. In most conversations, team players will speak first in terms of "we" as opposed to "I" even when they are answering direct questions about themselves.

Like the management team, the employees function as a team and must also develop chemistry to be efficient. Once the complete team is formed, the entrepreneur has to nurture and monitor the team's chemistry at the both the management and employee levels. One of the key detractors of chemistry is favoritism. The slightest hint of favoritism within the management or employee ranks will ruin the chemistry of the entire team. The entrepreneur must constantly guard against favoritism. Indifference, the opposite of favoritism, has the same dampening affect on team chemistry. In the formative years at TeleSynthesis, the management team hired the best employees available. Because they were the best available, TeleSynthesis management believed that they could function without direction. They were capable of performing their jobs without management intervention. The early TeleSynthesis managers left the employees to their own devices knowing they were the best athletes in the draft and they didn't need direction. While this is partially true, the employees viewed the approach as indifference. If management didn't care, then neither did the employees. This particular condition was hard to understand for the management team until TeleSynthesis hired a manager whose style wasn't one of indifference. The new manager's ability to build chemistry and, therefore, efficient teams was soon recognized and adopted by the entire company.

213

Building a fast-track vehicle requires precise organizational skill. It also requires good judgment concerning people, their abilities, and their personality traits. These skills coupled with a clear roadmap will have your company in the fast lane in no time.

Driving in the Fast Lane

Now that you have a roadmap and your vehicle is built, it's time for that all-important test drive. Unfortunately, even test-driving your vehicle can be difficult because sometimes you can't even get on the road. TeleSynthesis had trouble closing our first sale because we were a new business without a track record. To rectify the situation, TeleSynthesis leveraged the personal networks of the founders to secure our first customer. Our first sale was a real breakthrough in terms of our ability to market and sell the company's capabilities because it established TeleSynthesis as a viable business with a track record.

After landing our first deal, we believed the worst was behind us in terms of gaining traction. This proved to be true but, as is true with most test drives, we learned some surprising lessons about our vehicle. The most interesting lesson being we were unable to deliver software solutions efficiently. The problem wasn't TeleSynthesis per se. The problem was TeleSynthesis was following the generally accepted practices of the software development industry. These practices are very immature when compared to practices used to design and build structures in the physical world. TeleSynthesis, an immature company in an immature industry, in an effort to avoid being cut by this double-edged sword, revised our software development process to reflect the principles followed in the design and construction of structures in the physical world.

As TeleSynthesis came to understand, software projects, no matter how strongly software developers argue otherwise, are not executed in the

ADAPTING TO YOUR CUSTOMER

same mature, disciplined fashion as constructing a building. When compared to constructing buildings, software solutions are developed in an imprecise fashion akin to the process followed by people building barns a hundred years ago. In those times, a farmer needing a barn would simply invite his neighbors over to help him build it. The neighbors would bring their tools and literally build a barn from scratch, based on the group's collective understanding of a barn. Such barn building projects were completed successfully without attention to planning, specification, and design because the project was simple to understand and the neighbors where likely skilled craftsman.

While this method is effective for very simple projects, neither high-rise office buildings nor software can be built efficiently following this simple, immature process. When the desired software solution has the characteristics of a high-rise office building instead of a barn, the project must be defined and specified by an architect before it is engineered and built. This approach is rarely followed in developing software because the current industry mindset emphasizes the tools and technology necessary to build the solution over the definition of the solution. TeleSynthesis, in our first significant act of maturation, redefined our process to emphasize architecture instead of engineering.

The net result of our initial test drives as a company was we were constantly changing our vehicle. We initiated changes to TeleSynthesis based on our quest for efficiency, adjustments required by cycles in the business climate, and due to the maturation of our management team and organization. Change is a constant attribute of a growing, fast-tracking company.

Within three years of launching TeleSynthesis, we reached a period in which we felt we no longer needed to change. We knew the telecommunications market very well and our management team had gained significant business expertise. The vehicle we designed, built, and

215

subsequently refined was operating smoothly. Unfortunately, the telecommunications industry collapsed, and, in order to survive, we knew we needed to diversify into healthier markets. The diversification of the business brought about one of the most challenging changes TeleSynthesis faced.

In the telecommunications industry, our customers were engineers. For these engineers we built systems that interfaced with other computer systems in the telephone network. These systems had little or no end user interaction. When we diversified the business, we found we needed to be able to build computing systems that were used by people instead of other computing systems. To add to our dismay our new customers were less technical than the engineering customers we used to have. The new customers also needed a graphical interface to use the software systems we developed. Initially, our engineering staff had a difficult time working with this new type of customer. This difficulty came to light when a senior person in TeleSynthesis told the customer in a pre-sales meeting that he "hated user interfaces." Of course the customer quickly came to the conclusion that if we hated user interfaces, we'd hate their project and might even hate them. TeleSynthesis was not awarded any work on the customer's user interface until we recanted our declaration.

Reacting to the fall out caused by the comment taught us that to successfully diversify the company we needed to change our attitude. For the first time in the history of the company, we had to emphasize capabilities such as the ability to interact with end users over our engineering expertise. This was difficult for a company that was founded by engineers and had an employee base that was two-thirds engineers. But we realized that we had to reinvent the company to better serve different types of customers. Adapting to the change in customer types required only small changes to our engineering process but had far reaching implications in other areas of the business. We learned we had to reinvent most of the vehicle we had been driving. We changed our marketing message, our approach to sales, how we structured contracts, and how we defined the projects from the customer's perspective. We had lost the common ground we always shared with our telecommunications customers who were engineers, but we gained a broadened perspective of who we were, what we had to offer, and how we provided our services. Adopting these changes were the key to our successful diversification.

The take-away for the entrepreneur of a fast-tracking company is everything you can imagine and situations you can't imagine will drive changes. Your organization must be capable of adopting to changes. While the ability to change is useful, it creates a paradoxical situation for the company. The paradox is due to the fact that operating according to a well-conceived plan ensures overall efficiency and reacting to changes is inherently inefficient. Companies must strike a balance between reacting and planning. When you first start the company and are in your formative years, you are more likely to operate in a reactionary fashion. As the company matures your culture will become one that is less reactionary and more planning oriented.

In many aspects subjecting your company to change produces the same affect your body undergoes during physical training – it gets stronger. You must push constantly to be stronger, better, faster than the competition. A start-up company requires constant change to survive. Change is inherent in a start-up and it must be inherent in an established organization. The team and your organization must embrace change.

If you believe your company is mature but you find your organization constantly reacting to change, either your plans are inappropriate or your organization can't execute according to the plan. At TeleSynthesis, we found ourselves in a state of constant change that was brought on by our customers. We found that our unorganized, undisciplined customers disrupted our highly-disciplined approach to projects. They kept throwing us off track. At first we dismissed this condition based on the rationale that the customer is always right.

Eventually our customers began to point out that blindly following their every whim did not provide them with much value. In fact, this behavior actually cost them enormous sums of money. While we gladly collected large sums of money from our undisciplined customers, we found that this behavior did not build long-term relationships because customers believed they were paying us for more than just developing software, they felt they were paying us to protect them from themselves. Customers are often their own worst enemy because they will ask us to develop a feature or capability they want but they don't necessarily need. They rarely consider the cost of these frequent requests and are disappointed when the project comes in over budget and behind schedule. We changed our approach to dealing with our customers and began analyzing and explaining the return on investment the requested capability would yield. We would then allow the customer to decide if they wanted to make the investment in the capability. The revised approach has meant less near-term revenues for TeleSynthesis, but it helped us manage changes initiated by the customer and has helped TeleSynthesis build stronger, long-term relationships.

Because the culture and nature of the company is defined and controlled by the entrepreneur, the entrepreneur must be capable of recognizing the need to change and have the ability to act upon the change. Implementing change successfully requires a plan of what to change, how to effect the change, and a communication mechanism that explains the need for the change to customers and employees. The explanation of change must be clear and concise. Too many entrepreneurs just tell the affected people that it's their mandate and that's all they need to know.
When you are driving in the fast lane and you must make changes, make them carefully so you don't run over your customers or your employees in the process!

Toward the Finish Line

The vehicle you've built is speeding down the highway following your roadmap. You can make changes and adjustments effectively. Now what? If you are the inventor, chances are you have been working on developing the next big idea. If you are the entrepreneur, you are ready to turn the wheel over to a CEO to complete the drive so you can move on to the next opportunity to build a roadmap or a racecar. If you are the operations-minded CEO, you probably are appreciative of the opportunity to drive the vehicle created by the entrepreneur to transport the inventor's idea to reality. Once again, we see that specialization is in play.

There is one more aspect of fast-tracking that one must consider and that is luck. Luck, both good and bad, is an integral part of business. Having either type of luck is much like having an idea - it does not guarantee success or failure. Good luck must be exploited and bad luck must be overcome. How well you do this depends on how well you've designed and built the vehicle you are currently driving in the fast lane.

David Paul Taylor is the President and co-founder of TeleSynthesis, Inc. David has over 25 years of expertise and formal education in both traditional engineering and software engineering disciplines. David's technical and business background includes management, strategic planning, product architecture, and sales engineering responsibilities for companies such as Nortel Networks, Evolving Systems and Air Products.

"I'm an original thinker who excels at starting and organizing projects. The ability to complete projects does not come naturally to me", says David. "This proved to be problematic early in my career when people hired me with the expectation that I would complete specific tasks. Before I co-founded TeleSynthesis, I didn't realize that my creativity,

intuition, organizational skills and the ability to work from a clean slate made me a business architect. Now I'm thankful to be able to work with people whose personalities are the perfect complement to mine. That is to say, it's great to work with highly talented people who are able to finish what I start."

Lessons Learned through Perseverance

Jill Blashack
Tastefully Simple
Founder, CEO & President

Starting a Company: Perseverance

I have been in business for myself before with some success. First, I tried my hand at the restaurant business then moved to the tanning industry and then the gift basket business. Like every other business person, I had my highs and my lows, and, at every turn, the voice of reason would whisper, "Give it up, Jill. Get a REAL job." Yet when I started this business, I couldn't give up the dream of having something that mattered, something that could become a legacy.

Starting a business was never about money. If it had been, I would have jumped ship in those first few years of Tastefully Simple. I can only assume that this was also true for some of our earliest consultants, and I have the utmost respect for them. They persevered and some even turned their backs on high-profile corporate jobs. If I had been in their shoes, I don't know if I could have done it!

It's always a risk when we start a business. I took a risk when I chose to stay in, as did those early consultants. In order for me to persevere, it was important that I focus on what I could gain instead of focusing on what I stood to lose.

Recognize Your "Why"

People's reasons for starting a company are varied. Some people get into it for money, and some people get into it for recognition. For me, it's about the challenge and being able to tap my potential. Entrepreneurship is a perfect fit for people like me because we thrive on that challenge. We like the 'rush' we experience when we're creating something new and exciting. We like being a pioneer and being on the edge.

LESSONS LEARNED THROUGH PERSEVERANCE

I'm a random thinker. I can have countless thoughts running rampant through my mind at any given time. I have to force myself to focus. How would I do in a less chaotic work environment? Not well. While my life would drive many people to distraction, it is that very distraction that drives my life.

I'm also a generalist. I have a broad range of interests. As an entrepreneur, I can use that wide range of interests and talents to meet almost any challenge. And as the world forces specialization, I believe entrepreneurship is the last refuge and salvation for generalists who love to be challenged.

Key Approach #1: Least to Most

There are three key approaches, or philosophies, to starting a company that worked for us. The first was embracing the "least to most" philosophy.

Generally speaking, I am financially conservative and prefer to take the safe-but-sure approach. Don't get me wrong; I had big dreams. But if you start your business overcapitalized, it is hard both from a morale and financial standpoint to cut back if trouble hits. The same is true when people live beyond their means. In hard times, they'll have farther to fall, more to lose, and a worse attitude about it than those who have built a life through slow and steady gains. We started our business small and had nowhere to go but onward and upward. And we appreciated every little triumph along the way.

Tastefully Simple's founding story is a testament to 'least to most' and bootstrapping at its finest. Our initial investment was a mere $16,000 in cash and a $20,000 SBA loan. I worked from a rent-free shed on founding partner Joani Nielson's property. There were no bathroom

223

facilities or running water for the first eighteen months. It was cold in the winter and hot in the summer. Products were packed on top of a pool table. I was the sole consultant and responsible for booking parties and trying to convince others to join our team. I was not paid a salary and only had an income if I was conducting parties and building our team of consultants. Yet, with the approach of "least to most", we strictly adhered to a financial strategy that kept overhead low and growth potential high.

Key Approach #2: We Reserve the Right to Get Smarter

The next philosophy that worked for us was, "We reserve the right to get smarter." I believe the biggest thing that stops people from going outside their comfort zones and going for what they want is that they think they need to do it perfectly. I am living proof that you don't have to know a lot, yet you do need to have the willingness and the openness to learn. When we approach something with the attitude of, "We reserve the right to get smarter," we're willing to try new things and learn from our mistakes. We view mistakes as lessons learned rather than being embarrassed by what some people consider failure.

I can't say enough about what those seven little words, "We reserve the right to get smarter", have done for our company. First, there is an element of gentle humor about it that puts people at ease. Whenever the phrase is uttered, you always see a little smile play across the face of whoever hears it, even as they're learning how we screwed up. Humor opens ears to be able to hear like nothing else.

Second, it carries with it a tone of forgiveness; nothing is beyond redemption. That provided a great culture for us to grow in. If something goes wrong, we say, "We did this. We messed up. We are going to make it right." I think that most companies won't admit their mistakes and,

LESSONS LEARNED THROUGH PERSEVERANCE

instead, cover them up, and the tone is set for their employees. Just like children, they cover up because they fear getting "spanked" – no raise, no promotion, no forgiveness, no redemption.

Third, it promotes honesty and integrity. In January of 2002, I unveiled our principles; one of which was the Law of Realness. The Law of Realness says, "If we are authentic and humble, we build trust in ourselves and others." Being humble is about being honest with ourselves, our consultants, and our team members. It's easier to trust someone and trust a company when mistakes are acknowledged and forgiven. And it's easier to develop solutions and alternatives as a team when we trust one another.

Key Approach #3: Develop and Live by Core Values

The third approach was to develop and live by our core values. I know that sounds trite. After all, doesn't every company do that? Yet this was not a go-through-the-motions exercise. It was a serious exploration into our corporate character and consciousness. It was less about *what* we were doing, and more about *how* we were doing it and *why*. We cared. It was personal.

In the fall of 1997, our HQ team got together for an afternoon to ask ourselves what we did and did NOT want to be known for as a company. We had a whole wall full of Post-It notes. We used an affinity diagram to break those ideas into clusters and came up with Tastefully Simple's seven core values. Today, those core values are the pulse of Tastefully Simple. They are the heart and soul of the company. They truly drive our culture and every decision we make.

I've learned that it is essential to know the "why" behind a decision. If we don't, then it's probably not a good decision. Too many companies

225

set down their policy, and if anyone questions the policy, they say, "It's our policy; just deal with it." We need to be able to articulate why we are making a decision and whether it reflects our core values and who we want to be as a company. If not, then we reserve the right to get smarter. We let people know that we have messed up and we make the necessary changes.

Have Superb Products That Fill Needs

Along with these three key approaches, success is about selling a superb product that fills a need. Back in 1995, I certainly was clear about one thing. I knew that most people were busy and didn't have time to cook. Based on that belief, I defined the expectations of our product line: gourmet foods that were either open-and-enjoy products or were prepared by adding no more than two ingredients.

The need that I wanted to fill was the need for convenience. I knew that in my busy life, I didn't take time to cook. And I knew that gone were the days of ma and pa shops that catered to individual needs. Who chats anymore with the butcher about how to season a pot roast? Who do you call to find out how to make a glaze? Your mother? She's most likely at work and can't take your call!

Our products sell because they are superb AND they are convenient. They deliver the taste without the work. The seasoning is pre-mixed for the pot roast, and the glaze is in an easy-pour bottle. People buy products that fill their needs.

We also provide information in a fun environment. The premise of the home party business model is to provide one-to-one product knowledge. We took that one step further and provided our clients with the opportunity to EXPERIENCE the product, to be able to see, taste, smell, and touch it. This resulted in a fun, relaxed party. How relaxing is it to pick up your crabby kids at daycare and go to your local Jumbo Mart to grocery shop? Again, people buy products that fill their needs.

Can someone go to that Jumbo Mart, buy the appropriate ingredients, and eventually make what we sell? Possibly. Do most people want to? No. And they don't want to because they know that we offer convenience, as well as information and fun. Thirty years ago these needs relative to food did not exist, yet they are a reality of life today. The basic human needs of food, clothing, and shelter for that matter haven't changed, yet *how* humans live their lives inevitably dictates the way these things are delivered, now and in the future. Every entrepreneur starting out can benefit by asking themselves, "What is it I really deliver? How is my product or service unique and how does it reflect today's trends?"

Pitfalls

I don't believe any of us can be prepared for the risks and pitfalls of owning a business. Business ownership is a journey and a day-by-day education, one in which we often learn through trial and error and hindsight. As I've shared with our leadership team, "We all get up every day and figure it out as we go. Anyone who tells you they do it any other way is lying."

Here are some of the potential pitfalls that I have witnessed as an entrepreneur:

Pitfall #1: Succumbing to the Fear of Failure
I think the biggest risk for me was not as much financial as emotional. "What if this doesn't work and I have to admit that to people?" Those thoughts evoked fear in me. People would quite condescendingly ask,

"How is your little business doing?" and I would just smile and nod and say, "Oh, very well, thank you." Inside I was saying, "You just wait." I didn't know how I was going to get there, but I learned to use the fear of failure as a motivator.

Pitfall #2: Being Unresponsive

If I were to pick one thing that can often be the demise of a business, it's being closed to input and ideas. It is human nature for us to shut down if people question our paradigm. We don't want to hear it. It's important we listen with an open mind so we can learn what others are looking for.

I had an interview with someone we recently hired, and I asked him how he would drive sales. Louis said that he thought selling was really talking and listening to people and asking what they need. This type of receptiveness and open-mindedness is exactly what builds strong companies.

I'll be the first to admit that it's easy to become complacent and do things the same way because "it always worked before." But in the end, we run the risk that our consultants and clients will get bored, our leadership team will become timid, and other companies will spring up and pass us by.

Pitfall #3: Coddling Your Baby

Ironically, another risk in business can be success. Growth itself can be a huge threat: creating infrastructure, rapid hiring, communicating, maintaining a great culture, developing processes and procedures. Small companies have agility. In the beginning, I would take a project from start to finish. I came up with the product ideas. I talked with the vendors. I initiated the artwork and the labels and worked with Peg, our freelance graphic artist. I wrote the catalogue copy. I took product orders from our consultants. I had my hand in every detail of the business. Remember, by nature I'm a generalist!

Today, entire teams devote their time to those tasks. This was an important transition for me to make in order to ensure continued growth. As entrepreneurs, it can be very difficult to hand our baby over to others. We may tend to micromanage. I had a "spiritual awakening" when I was tweaking a team lead's writing project. I can guarantee you that it wasn't the first time! Lisa said to me, "Jill, I know that Tastefully Simple is your baby. It must be very difficult to turn your baby over to someone else."
She was right of course. It was time to turn over my growing baby. I learned through the school of hard knocks the importance of sharing my expectations with my team. I learned the importance of coaching them about how I think. It was critical to have a team that was willing to 'get inside my head', yet have the freedom to push back when they felt it necessary. Handing the details over to others freed me up to focus more on the big picture of Tastefully Simple and share our vision of where we were going.

Finding the Right People: Share Your Expectations

Another pitfall is not being clear about the kind of people you want to have on your team. The key to building a great business is hiring great people. I believe one of the ways that we have built a high caliber team is by creating our hiring process and systems with intent. We are clear in our expectations of our team members and we share these expectations in two ways.

First, we consistently state in our classified ads and our job descriptions the qualities that are desired for all team members. Specifically, all of our team members must be "team players", "positive", "ambitious", and "conscientious." This is not just lip service because our business philosophies rely heavily on individual team members to have fun while they produce results. The same is true for our leadership team. We seek leaders who are "visionary", "magic makers", "empowering", "passionate", "integrity-filled", and "results-oriented." These six attributes are non-negotiable and help us find leaders who resonate with our culture.

Second, we share our expectations through our job descriptions which are team buzzwords. If you wanted to join the communications team as a writer, for example, you would see the three buzzwords on the job description describing their team: "spirited," "efficient", and "professional." You would also see the team's undesirables: "missed deadlines", "inaccurate information", and "disrespect".

Once we attract potential team members, we use peer interviews. Key people who will be most involved with the new team member are part of the interview. This applies for every team member who comes on board, including leadership positions.

Inspiring the Team: Instill Your Culture

Once someone has joined our team, we work to inspire their commitment to our culture. First off, I need to confess that in the beginning, I didn't even know what our culture was. It has taken me time to figure it out and to have the ability to articulate what we stand for.

In 1996 and 1997, it was easy for Dolly and Joey, my two HQ team members, to understand what I believed in. Communication was much easier because it was "compressed" – we were within ear's shot of one another being in a 1,200 square foot shed! We didn't need a paging system or All-Team meetings. When I was taking an order, I would put the consultant on hold and just holler, "Hey, Joey, do we have some beer bread in stock?" Joey would shout back, "Yes," and then I would say, "We have beer bread, and we can ship that out for you right away."

I didn't have to worry about communicating our core values. After all, Dolly and Joey had been there when we developed them! As Tastefully Simple has grown, we have been challenged to maintain our culture and make sure that we are sharing our expectations with all of our team members. And as we add scores of consultants and headquarter's team members, we have to be confident that our core values are entrenched in the team.

Inspiring a culture of creativity and teamwork has been accomplished through some adopted business philosophies:

FISH!
We are very committed to the FISH! program created by Charterhouse Communications in Bloomington, MN, and train our team members and consultants on how to *Play, Be There, Make Their Day* and *Choose Your Attitude*. This philosophy creates a sense of personal responsibility to have fun while providing premium customer service.

Gung Ho!
In addition, our training and practice of the Gung Ho! business philosophy, introduced in the book of the same name by Ken Blanchard and Sheldon Bowles, provides a template for team empowerment that we've found invaluable.

Each of our teams operates almost like its own company and is held to the Gung Ho! standard of:

-Spirit of the SquirrelKnowing that our work is worthwhile
-Way of the BeaverBeing in control of achieving the goal
-Gift of the GooseCheering others on and seeking the positive

Gung Ho: Spirit of the Squirrel

When we believe that our work is worthwhile and that we make the world a better place, we come to work energized and engaged. Our team knows that they make a difference when we share emails from consultants about how their life has changed because of Tastefully Simple. They know their work is worthwhile when they attend our National Conference and see the tears of gratitude and the smiles of joy on the faces of our consultants. They know that they make the world a better place when their hard work contributes to the building of a home for Habitat for Humanity.

Gung Ho: Way of the Beaver

When people know that they are in control of achieving a goal, amazing things happen! In September, our leadership team goes away for two days for our annual Vision Retreat. We don't call it strategic planning. Who in the heck wants to go to a strategic planning meeting? Someone once said that Martin Luther King did not open his speech with "I have a strategic plan." The Vision Retreat is about dreams and goals and where we want to go as a company.

Following the Vision Retreat, every team schedules their Goal Post, a daylong, off-site retreat, where they determine their team's five Bold Steps and measurable goals for the year. These Goal Post retreats include either me or Vice President, Joani Nielson.

Halfway through the year, all of the teams revisit their Bold Steps to take stock of which goals have been reached and which need renewed attention. As each goal is reached, teams accumulate points toward monetary compensation as part of our Spirit of Success reward plan, a profit-sharing program. Even without this compensation, we know each team will set goals and will make great things happen. Everybody works together to make it happen. The team believes in the vision and they say, "Let's go for it." They have ownership. Tastefully Simple is THEIR business and they are very entrepreneurial. I believe the most effective teams are those that believe they are working toward something that benefits them as well as the company. They believe in what the company stands for. They realize they are a valuable part of our success. They know that their ideas will be welcomed and acted upon. I think many people feel isolated and disposable and are looking for ownership in their careers. It is important to give people an entrepreneurial mindset. This mindset not only allows them to do their jobs more effectively, it also helps them weather change and transition.

Gung Ho: Gift of the Goose
Cheering others on, seeking the positive and showing appreciation for great teamwork is priceless in creating a fun and nurturing work environment.

We have created daily rituals to celebrate small and large victories. For example, at 3:00 each afternoon, our Ambassador of First Impressions (in other companies they would be known as the receptionist) goes through each team ringing a brass bell, and shouting the number of new consultants that came on board that day. Sometimes it's a hundred consultants, sometimes it's ten, but we celebrate it all the same, with noisemakers, wolf whistles, and clapping. We also treat everyone to pizza as we hit pre-determined 'marker' goals along the way.

When we hit 3,500 consultants in 2001, Joani and I hand-delivered to every team member a jumbo chocolate bar with our victory printed on the wrapper along with a miniature brass bell. When we hit 10,000 consultants in 2002, we delivered a box of acorn-shaped chocolates and a stuffed squirrel with a tag that said, "Thank you for your worthwhile work."

We can have the most wonderful products, processes, or culture in the world, but if we don't move forward by getting other people involved, we will never make great things happen. Great things happen through teams, not individuals. There is selfishness, fear, and greed in much of our society that prevents teamwork, but when we allow our teams to reach their highest potential and soar, our success in business will soar with them.

The Lessons Learned

Tastefully Simple was built through trial and error. The lessons learned were a result of perseverance and choosing to focus on what could be gained, having something that mattered, and something that could become a legacy.

With her background in retail and business management and knack for bringing the right people and resources together, Jill Blashack is Founder, CEO and President of one of America's fastest growing privately held companies. Tastefully Simple is the original direct seller of convenience-driven gourmet foods through home taste-testing parties. As of 2002, Tastefully Simple had more than 10,000 independent consultants in 50 states and Puerto Rico and had product sales of $78 million.

From humble beginnings in 1995, Tastefully Simple has succeeded thanks to the amazing teamwork of Jill and Founding Partner, COO and Vice President, Joani Nielson, along with scores of consultants, as well as the headquarters' team in Alexandria, MN. In 2000, Jill was named the Ernst & Young Emerging Entrepreneur of the Year for Minnesota and the Dakotas. She has been quoted in the Wall Street Journal and Entrepreneur magazine. And last year, Inc Magazine ranked Tastefully Simple 7th on its prestigious Inc 500 list, a jump from 40th in its 2001 debut.

Jill and Joani remain true to their core values by 'nurturing the community in which they live', with 10 percent of after-tax profits supporting local causes, including a personal concern for the area's beautiful lakes and waterways.

Diving In –
The First Few Steps Are the Hardest

Doug Harrison
The Scooter Store
President & CEO

The Entrepreneurial Mindset

Build Something of Lasting Value
Part of the American dream is to be an entrepreneur, to create something – start it and run it – and have it be clearly one's own creation. It feels very good to be able to say, "This is my business." A very minor part of my entrepreneurial dream has anything to do with money. Success to me is measured by the substance of the business I have built, not its financial statement. As a father of three, I will always value my children based upon how they turn out as well-rounded adults, instead of based upon how much money they might make. Similarly, my entrepreneurial goal is to build a business that will be a well-rounded member of our democratic society. I am frequently asked about my future vision for the business. That is as hard for me as describing my future vision for my children. I have a simplistic plan in my mind for the future of my children that involves just a few basic steps like college, a challenging career, a loving spouse, happy children, and a sense of commitment and belonging to their community. In accomplishing those steps, I hope that my kids are honest, hardworking, and stick to their personal principles. My goals for our business aren't very different than that. I have a few basic steps in mind, but, mostly, I hope that we continue to be honest, hardworking, and stick to our core ideologies.

Personal Drive

I love to talk to other entrepreneurs, and I think that I have found a personal motivation that we all have in common. The entrepreneurs that I consider to be successful all have something to prove to someone. They all have different reasons, different things to prove, and different people to prove themselves to. One of the most difficult things that I have undertaken was to start to determine what my personal motivations are. Although most people see my business as an overwhelming success, I still am not satisfied, and I'm not sure why. Maybe if I am successful in determining what it is that really drives me, I will finally be able to describe what I consider to be personally successful. I think that if I ever get to that point, I may be able to be happier with my current level of success and not feel as driven to reach yet another level. I'm not sure if that's really a good thing or not.

Business Purpose

What I think is *not* common to successful entrepreneurs is an obsession with money that so many other business people seem to have. The ones I know who are just focused on money never become successful at building a very big business. Those who are focused on something else, such as building a big business for a higher purpose – a higher purpose than money – seem to be very successful. All the successful entrepreneurs I have known can tell you what their purpose is in running the business – and it is not a growth number, not a dollar number, it's something else. The day that we finally articulated, in writing, the mission statement for The SCOOTER Store is the day that we really started growing. Our business purpose is very easy to figure out. It's to help people in need of mobility, which is a cool purpose to have, and I love it and love working at it. There has to be a way for entrepreneurs to recharge their batteries, and stepping back from whatever today's emergency is long enough to contemplate our purpose seems to do it for me. Additionally, it allows me to quickly bring in lots of new people to drive growth and know that they will all be pulling in the same direction as the rest of the team. For the first several years of the business, I just assumed that employees would clearly be able to see what our mission was. However, the power of having it clearly defined in writing has been phenomenal. It makes business decisions easier, it makes goal setting easier, and best of all, it helps all the members of the team feel like they are connected to each other in a worthwhile endeavor.

Spotting Opportunity and Getting Started

Finding an Opportunity
Spotting opportunity is easy. You simply look around to see where people are not being served well. Or, as a consumer, ask what you would like to have available and where. When didn't you get the service or product you wanted? Those are business opportunities.

Spotting an opportunity for which you would be willing to risk everything you own is NOT easy. In fact, I think it is almost impossible. However, I don't think that should stop you from taking that risk. There is no such thing as a perfect opportunity. And, even if there was, someone would have already beaten you to it. I tell my employees all the time to love the impossibilities of their jobs. If the impossibilities didn't exist, someone much less qualified could fill their position. The impossibilities of picking the exact right business opportunity hold the same hidden blessing. Most people won't be willing to take the risk due to their fear that they're not making the right choice.

Taking the Plunge
In my opinion, opportunity is not the hard part; getting started is. Will the bungee cord of capitalism keep from crashing on the rocks after you jump off the edge? You'll never know if you don't jump. The decision my wife and I made to quit what we were doing was harder than almost anything else about running the business. Fear of the unknown and fear of failure nearly kept me from making the best decision of my life. My wife and I both quit our jobs, sold our house, moved into my parents' house, started the business, and immediately found out we were going to have our first baby – all in less than six weeks. In hind sight, all of that was easy compared to the decision to just do it.

My wife, my parents and I had spent a lot of time considering opportunities we had seen at business franchise shows, in the

240

newspapers, and so on. We finally picked two ideas we felt good about, because they had some real value – to us *and* to the community. The first one was a franchise of a company that offered rentals of wheelchair accessible vans. The second idea was a business called The SCOOTER Store that sells scooters and power wheelchairs, mainly for the elderly and disabled. We all thought that the van rental franchise would be our main business. As it turned out, that wasn't our best opportunity. We eventually closed that business to focus on selling scooters. Along the way we also discovered that we could be more helpful to our customers by offering a small power wheelchair, and now that is our main line of business.

Just Pick Something, Anything, and Then Take It From There.
Just like goal setting. You can never know if you picked the right goal, so you just pick one that is the most worthwhile at the time and DO IT. Then, when the next goal, the next opportunity, comes along, you have the confidence, mental discipline, and organizational support prepared to take advantage of the situation. In starting a business, you probably won't pick the right opportunity the first time, we certainly didn't, but who cares? Once you have a business started, any business, and it's your own, you will be much more likely to be able to take advantage of the big opportunity when it comes. If you are still plugging away at a job somewhere, you might not ever know what the opportunities are, much less when or how to pursue them.

Business Plan?

On a scale of one to ten, I'd give our business plan a one and a half. I really don't think the plan is very important – in our case it wasn't, anyway. If someone else is out to round up some venture capital money, I would assume they would have to have a slick business plan, but I don't know anything about that. We didn't start that way, and it meant we were never tied to it either. We started with a few ideas about what we wanted to do, what our business would do, who our customers would be – and we found out that we were wrong on just about every point. In fact, if we had written it down in more detail, it would have only meant that we were wrong with a lot more details. In the process of making our business work, we had to fail about nine times out of ten. So knowing what I know today, I wouldn't do those other nine things. Of course, that's a statement I can't apply to every entrepreneur. The only way I think a person starting a business is going to know what will work is to try all ten things. And each owner must figure out what feels right for his or her own motivation –and what feels right for the customers.

The part of creating a business plan that was valuable to me was the questions, not the finished product. The questions that we asked ourselves caused me to really think about why I wanted to be in this industry, and whether or not this was an opportunity that I could really believe in.

Essential Skills and Resources

Start-up Skills
The essential skills to start a business are very different than the essential skills necessary to make that business a big success. In the beginning, I had to learn that if something was worth doing, it was worth doing poorly, as long as it got done. Fine-tuning comes much, much later. To start a business you need absolute, bull-headed, stubborn determination. You must have the willingness to let go of a lot of ego and status and go do the work in the beginning. If a customer is mad about some little thing, you have to get in your car and go over and fix it. You have to be willing to say, "I'm going to do whatever it takes to make every customer satisfied."

Success Skills

I believe one of my essential skills for making the business successful was knowing when it was time to transition from good enough to great. In the beginning, great is the enemy of good. It is easy to never get projects (brochures, employee pay plans, store site selections, job descriptions, etc.) finished because they weren't completely perfect yet. Sometimes they weren't anything less than embarrassing, but we chose to proceed anyway, we had to proceed anyway. I think the reason is that in the beginning there is no "right" answer to many of the questions. So, you just choose one and move on. Later in the business, good becomes the enemy of great. If any issue becomes a repeat problem, or a repeat victory, and you settle for good enough, then you will never become GREAT! The trick is to not waste all of your time finding "great" solutions to problems and/or opportunities that will be irrelevant tomorrow.

However, the biggest single skill I think that I have that makes me successful as an entrepreneur is a love of people. I can't imagine how anyone could even hope to be successful as an entrepreneur if they don't absolutely love people, ALL people – customers, employees, vendors, legislators, community leaders, competitors, neighbors, EVERBODY! It's a people thing, so you have to love working with people, revel in their diversity, and love the challenge of figuring out how people react to situations, both on the employee side and on the customer side. It's like a puzzle. Why does that person feel that way, what makes them feel that way, and what can we do to make it different next time?

I have always loved talking to people, getting to know new friends, helping others resolve disagreements, and solve difficult problems. I eventually discovered that this was my favorite part of my job, my business, and my life. I believe this is the single largest factor that has driven my personal and professional success. I also clearly remember the times when I have failed at this task, and those times were my biggest personal and professional failures.

Other skills include the ability and desire to make the business "big" – having a good number of people working in it and a lot of customers who are being taken care of. A one or two-man shop with one or two customers isn't successful in my mind.

Resources

One resource I found to be extremely helpful was the Young Entrepreneurs' Organization (YEO). On a peer-to-peer level, networking and talking to other business owners was an eye-opener. Unquestionably, we wouldn't have made it without YEO. Before I got started in my new venture, I was an engineer and didn't know anything about running a business. It was through YEO that I learned how to run a business. As I look across my six person executive staff, it's notable that five of them came to me through contacts in the YEO network.

The Kauffman Center for Entrepreneurial Leadership is another amazing resource for anyone considering starting a new business. The group put out a CD called "How to Hire Awesome Employees." In my business, I thought every problem I had in the beginning was an employee problem. Then I received a copy of this CD and, come to find out, all it said about hiring awesome employees was just in the first sentence or two: It said awesome employees won't work for mediocre companies. If you have a mediocre company you can forget about ever attracting an awesome employee. It then went on to say how to build an awesome company, and I set out to follow that outline. There is now a book out from the Kauffman Center, entitled *Building an Awesome Organization,* which talks about everything that was on that original CD. If you think that you are even remotely interested in creating a business, I would recommend that you start by reading this book FIRST. You can find this along with

DIVING IN

an amazing array of other entrepreneurial learning at www.entreworld.org.

Running our business during high growth has an extremely unique set of challenges, too. We created an environment we called sustainable rapid growth. Every year, for our first ten years, we doubled or tripled in size. Assuming that you have taken the plunge, created a business, molded that into a profitable business model, and you are now ready to launch it into rapid growth mode, there is only one learning source I would recommend for you. Gazelles, Inc. is the firm run by Verne Harnish, the creator of YEO. He has the best tools I have ever found for practical, easy to implement basics of planning and operating a high growth business.

Managing Growth

So now you are growing. Go memorize Verne Harnish's book called the *Mastering the Rockefeller Habits*, or slow it down. Uncontrolled growth, with no plan, nearly killed us on several occasions. When a business is growing, whatever is done to trigger growth – usually revenue growth – is done at great risk. And care must be taken regarding a credibility risk with your own employees, as well as all other stakeholders.

Customer Service and Vision

Our customers are a bit unique. Ninety-nine percent of our customers are first time customers. The average life of the products we sell is about five years. Our average customer is seventy-seven years old and his or her life span is not five years out at that point. So we're constantly looking for new customers. Referrals are ten to fifteen percent of our sales, but for me, the importance of great customer care is not continued sales. The

245

INSIDE THE MINDS

importance is in fulfilling our mission that we have all committed to: To provide freedom and independence to people with limited mobility. Anything less than great service would risk betraying our mission and core values.

We have a customer care group that handles complaints, problems, or issues. The people in that department have been told they have unlimited funds to make each and every customer happy, and to right whatever it is the customer perceives to be wrong. No matter what the truth of any situation is, if the customer believes he or she has a problem, then there *is* a problem, and it must be resolved.

Because of the nature of our customers, it's easy to get our employees excited about the overall vision for the business. We help people who are literally prisoners in their own house become independent and mobile again. We encounter people who have given up on being able to do things on their own, and we get them into a scooter or power chair so they can do things again – from going out and getting the mail to being able to live independently. It's easy to get excited about giving someone's life back to him or her. Many of our customers have stories that would bring tears to your eyes, and getting them mobile is a neat thing to do. I love that side of it so much that it's easy to convince others to support the company's vision. First and foremost, I have bought into it. I have to love it the way I do, or I couldn't ask anyone else to be part of it.

We have a weeklong program called NEO (new employee orientation) for anyone joining the company. I tell each class my favorite customer story, which I can't tell without crying. The entire purpose of NEO is to help employees to learn and then buy into our shared vision from their first day on the job.

246

Building a Multi-Talented Team

What I need in my top management team is a mix of skills. I have tried to make a point of not having people with the same personality traits and skills and talents. We are a pretty odd bunch – by design. We have a team member who is adamant about keeping us focused on details and having all the processes in place. Another person can go ten million miles an hour and change everything, which keeps us from getting stuck in our ways for too long. One person is great at the relationship side of business – and life. He is a good people person. One is our strategic thinker, always planning and intellectualizing our business style. Our voice of experience and reality is an individual who frequently says, "Hey, wait a minute. I hear what you are saying, but let's be realistic about this." It is very important that the team has that spread of talent, each member with his or her own unique special skills.

Training Together
We have made a conscious decision to take my entire executive staff off-site at least twice per year for some type of business-related training. The idea generation has been incredible. We go off-site quarterly for a planning meeting, too, but those meetings are very focused on setting goals for the next quarter. We also do lots of social trips with the whole group to celebrate a victory or to just have fun. However, along with the value of additional, continuous training, something magic happens when the whole exec team is away together to think and learn. The intensity and the power of the thinking in those meetings continues to shape virtually every major decision in our business.

Meeting Rhythm
We have a VERY structured process of annual, quarterly, monthly, weekly, and daily meetings. We follow the formula from Verne's book almost to the letter. To get this structure of meetings put in place was originally very difficult. Now that we have it, none of us can imagine

living without it. The meeting rhythm allows us to relax and feel confident that we are doing the right things for the right reasons.

Playing Together

It is very important to me that our Executive team enjoys being with each other. No one is allowed to be a part of the team if the rest of the team is not comfortable spending time with them socially, as well as professionally. We have several trips a year to go away and play together. Some of those trips are with spouses, and some are just the execs. I believe that it is very important for us to be able to like each other so that we can trust each other. At the very foundation of our teamwork is trust.

Be nice

An outside recruiter recently told me that he finally figured out what it took to be a member of our exec team. He had identified all of the basic skills and experience, but we were still missing something. After spending more time with all of us, he told me he finally realized that to really fit in, any candidate would need to be a "nice" person. I don't know that I have ever been able to say it quite so succinctly, but that is really the core of it to me – the leaders of our company need to be nice people.

Complete honesty

Sometimes we fall into the trap of being so nice that we are not honest with each other. As long as you are careful about how you present an issue, I always believe that you can deliver absolute, blunt honesty and still be nice about it. The better my team has become about nice, but still completely honest with each other, the better we have performed. There have been many occasions when we weren't honest with each other, usually in a tough meeting, because we didn't want to embarrass a team member. Every time we have avoided what felt like a dangerous issue, we have caused a much worse problem down the road.

Communication Protocol

One of the best things that I learned in YEO was Communication Protocol. In YEO I had the opportunity to meet monthly with a small group of other entrepreneurs in a small group called a Forum. Inside the Forum, we were able to talk to each other in complete confidence and complete honesty. The single largest tool that enabled this to happen is called Communication Protocol. In the Forum meeting, you are not allowed to give advice, you can only speak from personal experience, and you have to offer a positioning statement before asking any question. My Forum became a safe haven for me that allowed me to talk about ideas and learn from other entrepreneurs. I liked the idea so much that I had my entire Exec team go through Forum Training. Our weekly Exec meeting is now structured around a rough outline of a Forum meeting. The level of open, honest, productive communication has increased dramatically. I already thought that the team worked well together, but now it is even better.

In 1991 the entrepreneurial spirit took over Doug Harrison's life and changed it forever. He and his wife, Susanna, were successful Yuppies living in New Orleans. Doug had worked for Conoco for only five years. A little success, a little luck, and a lot of determination had brought him to be the lead project engineer on Conoco's most advanced, revolutionary, and deepest offshore oil platform in the world. It was a dream job for a petroleum engineer; but somehow he wanted more. Susanna had gone from an office assistant at Computerland to the Director of Training for a software training company, Executrain, in less than two years; but somehow she wanted more, as well.

They began planning their future. They were (and still are) deeply in love and they wanted to spend more time together. They wanted to be back in Texas. They wanted to run their own business, and they really wanted the business to have a major positive impact on their community

INSIDE THE MINDS

and their customer's lives. In March of 1991 they decided that there would never be a "perfect" time for this major life change, so they decided to "Just do it!" Over just six weeks, they quit their jobs, sold their house, moved home to Texas and into Doug's parent's summerhouse, started the business, and found out that Susanna was pregnant.

Today, The Scooter Store, with 40 locations in 26 states, has well over 1000 employees, and is the largest private employer in all of Comal county. The Scooter Store's annual revenues have doubled or tripled for 9 out of 11 years in business. The Scooter tore has been on the Inc 500 list for the last three years, and Doug has been awarded the E&Y Entrepreneur of the Year Award.

Doug graduated from the Colorado School of Mines in 1986 with a degree in Petroleum Engineering. Doug and Susanna have three children, ages 6, 9 and 11. Doug has served on the Board of the New Braunfels Rotary Club, the McKenna Hospital Advisory Board, the San Antonio Multiple Sclerosis Society Board, the New Braunfels Eden Home board, and as President of the San Antonio Chapter of the Young Entrepreneurs Organization. He is still an active member of YEO (Young Entrepreneurs Organization) and YPO (the Young Presidents Organization).

WHAT EVERY EXECUTIVE NEEDS TO KNOW

Subscribe Today & Get Any Book Published by Aspatore For Free

Only $47.46/Year – 4 Quarterly Issues (30% Off Cover Prices)

C-Level Business Review is a quarterly management review, written by the world's leading executives. Each issue features the thinking of C-Level (CEOs, CFOs, CTOs, CMOs, Partners) executives from over 100 of the world's largest companies, not third party authors or columnists, so the information is pertinent and direct. *C-Level Business Review* provides you with information on the core areas every executive needs to be aware of, including management, technology, marketing, finance, operations, innovation, ethics, human resources and more - from the people who know. *C-Level Business Review* is your filter to learn more in less time. Be a thought leader, stay ahead of the curve and gain an edge. Subscribe today to *C-Level Business Review* for only $47.46 a year and get any book published by Aspatore for free (up to a $49.95 value all by itself).

Praise

"Want to know what the real leaders are thinking about now? It's in here." - Carl Ledbetter, SVP & CTO, Novell

"What C-Level executives read to keep their edge and make pivotal business decisions..." - Richard Costello, Manager-Marketing, General Electric

"A must read…." - Dr. Chuck Lucier, Chief Growth Officer, Booz-Allen & Hamilton

"Tremendous insights..." - James Quinn, Litigation Chair, Weil Gotshal & Manges

"An incredible resource…to help you develop outside-the-box..." - Rich Jernstedt, CEO, Golin/Harris Intl.

To Order or For Customized Suggestions From an Aspatore Business Editor, Please Call 1-866-Aspatore (277-2867) Or Visit www.Aspatore.com

ASPATORE BOOKS

Bulk/CUSTOMIZED BOOK Orders

Aspatore Books offers discount pricing and customization of cover art and text on bulk orders. Customization choices might include but are not limited to: Adding your logo to the spine and cover; Personalizing the book title to include your company's name; Removing specific unwanted content; Adding a letter from your CEO or others; Including an application form or other collateral materials. Companies use Aspatore books for a variety of purposes, including: Customer Acquisition, Customer Retention, Incentives and Premiums, Employee and Management Education. Contact Rachel Pollock at 617.742.8988 or rp@aspatore.com for more information.

LICENSE Content

Aspatore content is often licensed for publications, web sites, newsletters and more. Electronic licenses are also available to make an entire book (or series of books) available for employees and/or customers via your web site. Please contact Jason Edwards at jason@aspatore.com for more information.

Advertise in C-Level Business Review

Every quarter, C-Level Business Review reaches thousands of the leading decision makers in the United States. Subscribers to the magazine include C-Level executives (CEO, CFO, CTO, CMO, Partner) from over half the Global 500 and top 200 largest law firms. Please email jonp@aspatore.com for advertising rates and more information.

Corporate Publishing Group
(An Aspatore Owned Company)

Corporate Publishing Group (CPG) provides companies with on-demand writing and editing resources from the world's best writing teams. Our clients come to CPG for the writing and editing of books, reports, speeches, company. For more information please e-mail rpollock@corporateapublishinggroup.com.

To Order or For Customized Suggestions From an Aspatore Business Editor,
Please Call 1-866-Aspatore (277-2867) Or
Visit www.Aspatore.com

GROW YOUR BUSINESS LIBRARY

Subscribe to Aspatore Books

40 Books of Your Choice a Year – Only $699
(Over 50% Savings)

The *Aspatore Books Subscription* features must-have business books spanning all industries and professions, offering a wealth of information on crucial topics of timely importance – making for the ultimate resources for business professionals. Twice each year you will receive updates about new Aspatore Books available. Select 20 books every six months (you may also elect to pick multiple copies of the same book, or have an editor make the selections for you). Each book delivers industry intelligence from C-Level executives (CEO, CTO, CFO, CMO, CFO, Managing Partner) representing the world's most-respected companies. This collection is a highly valuable resource for easy-to-access, business intelligence from industry insiders on a tremendous range of topics (including management, innovation, technology, marketing, venture capital, financial services, law and over 30 industries). Each year, Aspatore Books publishes C-Level executives from over half the Global 500, top 250 professional services firms, fastest growing 500 private companies, law firms (MPs/Chairs), and other leading companies of all sizes.

Call 1-866-Aspatore and select 20 books from the following pages, or have an Aspatore Business editor select them for you.

To Order or For Customized Suggestions From an Aspatore Business Editor, Please Call 1-866-Aspatore (277-2867) Or Visit www.Aspatore.com

Best Selling Books

Visit your local bookseller today or visit www.Aspatore.com
for retail locations carrying Aspatore books.

Reference

Business Travel Bible – Must Have Phone Numbers, Business Resources & Maps
The Golf Course Locator for Business Professionals – Golf Courses Closest to
Largest Companies, Law Firms, Cities & Airports
Business Grammar, Style & Usage – Rules for Articulate and Polished Business
Writing and Speaking
ExecRecs – Executive Recommendations For The Best Business Products &
Services
Executive Zen – Mental & Physical Health & Happiness for Overworked
Business Professionals
The C-Level Test – Business IQ & Personality Test for Professionals of All
Levels
The Business Translator-Business Words, Phrases & Customs in Over 65
Languages

Management

Corporate Ethics – The Business Code of Conduct for Ethical Employees
The Governance Game – Restoring Boardroom Excellence & Credibility in
America
Inside the Minds: Leading CEOs – CEOs Reveal the Secrets to Leadership &
Profiting in Any Economy
Inside the Minds: The Entrepreneurial Problem Solver – Entrepreneurial
Strategies for Identifying Opportunities in the Marketplace
Inside the Minds: Leading Consultants – Industry Leaders Share Their
Knowledge on the Art of Consulting
Inside the Minds: Leading Women – What It Takes to Succeed & Have It All in
the 21st Century
Being There Without Going There: Managing Teams Across Time Zones,
Locations and Corporate Boundaries

Technology

Inside the Minds: Leading CTOs – The Secrets to the Art, Science & Future of
Technology
Software Product Management – Managing Software Development from Idea to
Development to Marketing to Sales
Inside the Minds: The Telecommunications Industry – Leading CEOs Share
Their Knowledge on The Future of the Telecommunications Industry
Web 2.0 AC (After Crash) – The Resurgence of the Internet and Technology
Economy
Inside the Minds: The Semiconductor Industry – Leading CEOs Share Their
Knowledge on the Future of Semiconductors

Venture Capital/Entrepreneurial

Term Sheets & Valuations – A Detailed Look at the Intricacies of Term Sheets &
Valuations

To Order or For Customized Suggestions From an Aspatore Business Editor,
Please Call 1-866-Aspatore (277-2867) Or
Visit www.Aspatore.com

Deal Terms – The Finer Points of Deal Structures, Valuations, Term Sheets, Stock Options and Getting Deals Done

Inside the Minds: Leading Deal Makers – Leveraging Your Position and the Art of Deal Making

Hunting Venture Capital – Understanding the VC Process and Capturing an Investment

Inside the Minds: Entrepreneurial Momentum – Gaining Traction for Businesses of All Sizes to Take the Step to the Next Level

LEGAL

Inside the Minds: Privacy Matters – Leading Privacy Visionaries Share Their Knowledge on How Privacy on the Internet Will Affect Everyone

Inside the Minds: Leading Lawyers – Leading Managing Partners Reveal the Secrets to Professional and Personal Success as a Lawyer

Inside the Minds: The Innovative Lawyer – Leading Lawyers Share Their Knowledge on Using Innovation to Gain an Edge

Inside the Minds: Leading Labor Lawyers – Labor Chairs Reveal the Secrets to the Art & Science of Labor Law

Inside the Minds: Leading Litigators – Litigation Chairs Revel the Secrets to the Art & Science of Litigation

Inside the Minds: Leading IP Lawyers – IP Chairs Reveal the Secrets to the Art & Science of IP Law

Inside the Minds: Leading Deal Makers – The Art of Negotiations & Deal Making

FINANCIAL

Inside the Minds: Leading Accountants – The Golden Rules of Accounting & the Future of the Accounting Industry and Profession

Inside the Minds: Leading Investment Bankers – Leading I-Bankers Reveal the Secrets to the Art & Science of Investment Banking

Inside the Minds: The Financial Services Industry – The Future of the Financial Services Industry & Professions

Building a $1,000,000 Nest Egg – 10 Strategies to Gaining Wealth at Any Age

Inside the Minds: The Return of Bullish Investing

Inside the Minds: The Invincibility Shield for Investors

MARKETING/ADVERTISING/PR

Inside the Minds: Leading Marketers–Leading Chief Marketing Officers Reveal the Secrets to Building a Billion Dollar Brand

Inside the Minds: Leading Advertisers – Advertising CEOs Reveal the Tricks of the Advertising Profession

Inside the Minds: The Art of PR – Leading PR CEOs Reveal the Secrets to the Public Relations Profession

Inside the Minds: PR Visionaries – PR CEOS Reveal the Golden Rules

Inside the Minds: Textbook Marketing – The Fundamentals We Should All Know (And Remember) About Marketing

To Order or For Customized Suggestions From an Aspatore Business Editor, Please Call 1-866-Aspatore (277-2867) Or Visit www.Aspatore.com

Inside the Minds:
JumpStart

Acknowledgements and Dedications

Penny Baker – Dedicated to my wife and business partner, Amy Baker and also to Pete Estep, Trey Dolezal and my father, Penny Baker Sr. I'd like to acknowledge Barbara Wray, Austin-Tex.-based freelance writer for her assistance.

James R. Barnes - Dedication - To my Uncle Joe, Joseph Ravalese Jr., who taught me very strong principles of basic business. I am reminded when I hop on a plane of his tie clip with the abbreviation: YCDBSOYC (You can't do business sitting on your can). As well as the framed saying on his office wall; "Once you give up integrity, everything else is a piece of cake". I also very much remember him spending 45 minutes on the phone once saving a customer from canceling who was paying $12 per month. He explained and I later understood that it was $12 this month, next month, and each month of each year and so forth and so on. Thank you for taking me in under your wing.

Jill Blashack – I dedicate this chapter to the memory of my late husband Steven Blashack "for his encouragement and faith in Tastefully Simple" as well as my parents, Jean Schmitz and John Schmitz, "for the pain they have endured with courage and faith and for always believing in me." I would like to thank Christine Nelson and Janet Dullinger for their contributions to this article.

David Carlson - To my co-founders – John Imrie, Ken Polk and Michael Taggart and to my wife Lenora who was always supportive of my entrepreneurial ideas.

Kevin Grauman - I would like to dedicate this chapter to my late father, for teaching me: To never accept the status quo; To think outside of the box; To challenge absolutes; To always have a "fly on the wall" perspective; and to do so ethically and with unrivalled integrity.

Marina Hatsopoulos – Dedicated to George Hatsopoulos, Walter Bornhorst, and in memory of Don Noble.